DUI–
Destiny
Under
the Influence

How Satan Is Attempting to Turn God's
Glorious Bride into a Drunken Harlot

Jeremiah C. Merritt

WestBow
PRESS
A DIVISION OF THOMAS NELSON

In conducting research, the author utilized the Bible app for YouVersion (smartphone app version
4.0.13) to access multiple translation versions of the Bible. See http://www.youversion.com.

Scripture taken from the King James Version of the Bible.

WestBow Press books may be ordered through booksellers or by contacting:

WestBow Press
A Division of Thomas Nelson
1663 Liberty Drive
Bloomington, IN 47403
www.westbowpress.com
1-(866) 928-1240

ISBN: 978-1-4497-8586-4 (sc)
ISBN: 978-1-4497-8585-7 (hc)
ISBN: 978-1-4497-8587-1 (e)

Library of Congress Control Number: 2013903097

Printed in the United States of America

WestBow Press rev. date: 2/27/2013

CONTENTS

Preface.. ix

Introduction... xi

Chapter 1. The Holy Spirit and a Sleeping Spirit......................... 1

Chapter 2. Sleepers and Sinners Wind Up in the Same Boat 11

Chapter 3. God's Wake-Up Call.. 19

Chapter 4. Jesus Is Coming like a Thief in the Night.................... 29

Chapter 5. A Drunken Sleep 39

Chapter 6. Mixed Drinks Will Leave You Mixed Up 43

Chapter 7. All Worship Isn't Welcome....................................... 53

Chapter 8. The Music Is Magic 63

Chapter 9. What's behind Your Worship?................................... 69

Chapter 10. Don't Lose the Head in Your Dance......................... 77

Chapter 11. True Worship Is Found at the Well 83

Chapter 12. The Church Can't Use Flesh Hooks! 93

Chapter 13. We Can't Have God's Presence and Hemorrhoids............. 109

Chapter 14. Worship That Ushers In God's Presence.................... 117

Conclusion.. 131

My deepest appreciation to:

My wife, Tifani, who is totally priceless to me. I thank the Lord daily for giving me a true helpmeet, who has been with me every step of the way in life and ministry. Outside of the "Comforter" (the Holy Spirit), there is no greater comfort than to have her beside me as we fulfill God's call on our lives.

My four children, Jeremiah Jr., Taylor, Joseph, and Josiah. You are truly a gift from God. Thank you for sharing your dad with the body. I love you dearly.

My church family of Kingdom Life Ministries of Darlington. I thank God for the flock that he has given me to watch over. Without all of you, this book wouldn't be possible, as the book in its entirety comes from the many teachings preached to all of you. I love you.

Preface

In the summer of 2009, God dealt with me intensely, through prayer and study, about the deceptive nature of the Enemy and about how he uses valid spiritual necessities like praise and worship to release his deceptive poison into the body of Christ. God immediately had me launch the series "DUI—Destiny Under the Influence" in my local congregation. This series intensely impacted us all and opened our eyes to the depths of the purging that must take place in the body of Christ. Week after week, the Holy Spirit unfolded to us the realization of how Satan has used praise and worship to intoxicate the body of Christ and move us away from worshipping Christ and back to worshipping a calf (a form of godliness). In the midst of this teaching, the Spirit of the Lord spoke clearly to me that he was writing a book while I was teaching this series. He told me that this word must be published and used as a perfecting work for his body.

Most of the concepts and principles in this book were first taught in presentations to a live audience; it has been extremely difficult to transfer them into a written form that carries the necessary fluency so readers who haven't been exposed to the topic can grab ahold of it. This book doesn't follow all of the conventional styles of writing and format, for it was not planned out before it was written. It was written week by week as the Holy Spirit moved upon my spirit. Although the writing style may not be what you're accustomed to, I promise that as you read it with the help of the Holy Spirit there will be a revolution that takes place in your spirit-man.

I want to thank Kingdom Life Ministries of Darlington, the church in which I am the senior pastor, for receiving the message in this book not as the word of man, but as it is in truth, the word of God.

Introduction

One thing that the Bible makes clear is that in the last days, one of the main demonic spirits that will be unleashed against the saints is the spirit of slumber. We can deduce this because several passages make it clear that many if not most believers will have a very difficult time remaining spiritually awake. Not only that—the Bible says that many saints will literally, actually fall asleep.

In the gospel of Matthew, Jesus states over and over the necessity of his disciples to maintain a spiritual awareness, and more so, not to fall asleep, because when he returns, it will be at a time when the world least expects it (see Matt. chapter 24). After giving his disciples this sobering warning, he tells the parable of the ten virgins—five wise and five foolish. Jesus deals exclusively with his return in this story.

There are a few things we should note about this parable. First, they were all virgins, meaning they were pure. Second, while the bridegroom (representing Jesus) tarried, they all slumbered and slept. (Matt. 25:5) What is the Lord attempting to communicate to his church? It's this: Just because you're not living in blatant sin doesn't mean you're spiritually awake!

The gospel of Matthew also shows Jesus in the Garden of Gethsemane, when he was living out his final moments of his earthly life and was about to close out his earthly ministry. His last days on earth point prophetically to the last days of earth. The main priority Jesus wanted to establish in his followers—his disciples—at Gethsemane was prayer. "Watch and pray, that ye enter not into temptation: the spirit indeed is willing, but the flesh is weak" (Matt. 26:41). The issue was that when Jesus looked for his closest disciples—Peter,

James, and John—to pray for him in his last days, he found them sleeping. Jesus woke them up and said, "Stay awake and pray that you will not fall into temptation" (Matt. 26:41 NET). Jesus went back and prayed to accept his Father's will. Then he returned to his closest disciples: "And he came and found them asleep again: for their eyes were heavy" (Matt. 26:43). They couldn't remain awake!

We're living in a day and age when God's power visits us through worship, the Word, and divine touches from the Master that awaken us. God places in us an urgency to answer our high priestly calling of intercession, persistent prayer, and walking in the Spirit. But sadly, just like the disciples in the Garden of Gethsemane, after the Holy Spirit wakes us up, when he comes back, he finds us sleeping again—indifferent and insensitive to the leading of the Holy Spirit.

Notice that these disciples were not just carnal Christians who had fallen asleep on Jesus when he needed their intercession and prayer the most. These three disciples—Peter, James, and John—were those closest to the Messiah. Now, we're living in the last days, a time in which the spirit of slumber has taken its toll, and sadly, even many of those men and women who are closest to Jesus have fallen asleep and need to be awakened again! We have turned from prayer and intercession to promotion, programs, and conferences. This book is for every Peter, James, and John out there who must be awakened again in these last and evil days.

Just as the first disciples had the responsibility to pray Jesus through one of his final hours before he left the earth, we who are his last disciples hold the responsibility of praying for Jesus in this final hour before his imminent return. There is one thing that stands in our way: the spirit of slumber. Jesus came and found his first disciples asleep, because their eyes were heavy—in other words, they couldn't keep their eyes open. On a spiritual level, we have a similar challenge in the body of Christ today: we don't know how to keep our spiritual eyes open!

The reason why we have such a problem with the spirit of sleep and slumber is because the Enemy has gotten us to confuse rest with sleep. Jesus is the

Lord of the Sabbath, the Lord of rest. As God calls us into his rest, the Enemy perverts God's rest to get us to fall into sleep! The enemy has gotten us to choose sleep, when we should instead rest. The difference between sleep and rest is great. When you're asleep, you close your eyes and are unconscious; when you're at rest, your eyes are open and you are still at watch. We are never to close our spiritual eyes. The Holy Spirit doesn't rest—he gives rest. Many saints don't understand that you can have your natural eyes open and your spiritual eyes closed!

Believers often don't recognize they are spiritually asleep although they are awake and active in the natural world. We can be asleep in the spirit with our natural eyes wide open—a form of sleepwalking. The church's issue isn't that she's not *walking*; we have plenty of activities, youth and children programs, marriage ministry, singles' ministry, and the list goes on. The problem is that many times we're sleepwalking! We're doing works, not understanding how the Enemy is acting against us, not knowing whether our works find their origin from heaven.

Chapter 1

The Holy Spirit and a Sleeping Spirit

The Spirit of Slumber Is Prevalent in the Last Days—It's Not about the Holy Spirit Coming, It's about Him Staying

In order to understand the spirit of slumber and how it affects us, we've got to look at how God's Holy Spirit interacts with our reborn spirit when we're saved. God's Holy Spirit will have fellowship and communicate with only our reborn spirit. He refuses to fellowship directly with our soul or body. That is key in understanding how the Enemy causes our spirit to slumber.

When John the Baptist was baptizing in the Jordan, he said,

I saw the Spirit descending from heaven like a dove, and it remained on him [Jesus]. And I knew him not: but he that sent me to baptize with water, said unto me, upon whom thou shalt see the Spirit descending, and remaining on him, that's the one who baptizes with the Holy Ghost (John 1:32–33).

John knew Jesus was the Messiah, not because the Holy Spirit came upon him, but because the Holy Spirit remained on him. The Holy Spirit comes upon many of us too, but he doesn't remain on many of us. Whether we're asleep or awake in the Spirit depends not on whether the Holy Spirit has come upon us but on whether the Holy Spirit remains and takes residence in us. It all hinges on the Holy Spirit.

The Holy Spirit came upon Jesus in the form of a dove. Why? Because the dove speaks of the Holy Spirit's nature. A dove is a timid bird that can easily be startled and scared away. If a dove ever lands near you, it's so important that you're quiet, that you don't make sudden movements or do anything to draw attention to yourself, because if you do, the dove will fly away! What's the revelation? We've got to be sensitive to the Holy Spirit! How? By not living life focused on ourselves. Just like a dove will fly away if we draw attention to ourselves, the Holy Spirit will lift if we're living a self-focused life. "If any man will come after me, let him deny himself, and take up his cross, and follow me" (Matt. 16:24). Anytime we're living self-focused or self-centered, we're walking in offense to the Spirit of God. When we offend him, he won't stay! He's like a dove; we've got to make sure we walk carefully, living a life of self-denial, so we won't be offensive to him.

The letter to the Ephesians says to "walk circumspectively" (Eph. 5:15), or in other words, walk cautiously. We've got to be careful not to live self-indulgent, self-pleasing lifestyles. Our lives must be built around knowing and serving Jesus, not ourselves. Otherwise we'll live inconsistently in regard to walking in the Spirit. So many in the church today don't live lives in the Spirit, because preachers preach a self-focused gospel, prophets prophesy self-focused prophecies, and believers come to hear a self-focused message. Very few in the church are led by the Spirit—most are self-focused instead of God-focused. Paul lamented the time when the church would lose the ability to walk in the Spirit when he said, "This know also, that in the last days perilous times shall come. For men shall be lovers of their own selves" (2 Tim. 3:1–2). He says that they "will be lovers of pleasures more than lovers of God" (2 Tim. 3:4). Because we live in a church age in which people love self and pleasure more than God, we have a baby boom of Christians who haven't the slightest clue what it means to walk in the Spirit and who, if they don't repent, will be victims of the satanic slumber that is so prevalent in today's church. We must understand that to walk in the Spirit is to walk in sensitivity to him, by denying ourselves daily, taking up our cross, and following Jesus (see Luke 9:23). The Holy Spirit is like a dove—we must be ever sensitive to him, or he'll leave.

The Holy Spirit Only Wants Jesus

Jesus says of the Holy Spirit:

Nevertheless I tell you the truth; It is expedient for you that I go away: for if I go not away, the Comforter will not come unto you; but if I depart, I will send him unto you. And when he is come, he will reprove the world of sin, righteousness, and judgment … Howbeit when he, the Spirit of truth, is come, he shall guide you into all truth: for he shall not speak of himself; but whatsoever he shall hear, that shall he speak … He shall glorify me: for he shall receive of mine, and shall shew it unto you (John 16:7–15).

In other words, Jesus says this about the Holy Spirit: "He shall never speak of himself … he shall speak of me only. He'll take what is mine and show it to you." What Jesus is helping us understand is that the Holy Spirit is single in his focus; he exists in us for Jesus alone! He will have fellowship with us on the basis of Jesus Christ only.

Our human spirit can only have fellowship with God's Holy Spirit in regard to Jesus Christ. What this means is that when we were reborn, we received from God a regenerated spirit created to have fellowship with God's Holy Spirit. This fellowship's sole purpose is to reveal Jesus Christ to us. "He [the Holy Spirit] will honor and glorify Me, because He will take of (receive, draw upon) what is Mine and will reveal (declare, disclose, transmit) it to you" (John 16:14 AMP). Our born-again spirit is wired by God to want only Christ. Jesus is the only reason we receive a regenerated spirit.

The Enemy puts our spirit to sleep by getting us to be interested in things that our regenerated spirit has no interest in. Remember, our born-again spirit wants only Christ. Satan works over time to get us tied into things that have nothing to do with Christ—activities, events, hobbies, and pastimes that aren't Christ-centered, but self-centered. Watching secular movies and secular television, having unrighteous conversations and connections, and overindulging in Internet interactions through Facebook and Twitter are all means by which the Enemy puts our spirit to sleep, with seemingly innocent activities!

Lust Will Always Make Love Leave

The first epistle of John says, "Love not the world, neither the things that are in the world … For all that is in the world, the lust of the flesh, the lust of the eyes, and the pride of life, is not of the Father, but is of the world" (1 John 2:15–16). It also says that "the whole world lieth in wickedness" (1 John 2:19). The Bible makes it clear that everything in the world that doesn't find its source in God—secular movies, secular television, secular Internet—carries within it the spirit of lust. God in the person of the Holy Spirit is love. Lust and love can't co-exist, just like flesh and spirit can't co-exist. Lust will always cause love to lift. The Holy Spirit won't remain with us in an environment in which we're gratifying the lust of our own flesh or eyes. The Bible talks about not grieving the Holy Spirit (see Eph. 4:30). When we indulge in lust, the Spirit of God is grieved, because he has to leave!

Any time that we willingly partake of lust, love leaves!

When we willingly place the Holy Spirit of God in environments in which we are compromising or self-indulging, such as where we are partaking of the lusts of this world, the spirit of God lifts like a dove does. Believe it or not, our regenerated spirit only wants to hear about Jesus, not about us! When we focus on self, the Holy Spirit—the only one who shows Jesus to us—will leave. Once the Holy Spirit lifts, our spirit has nothing to feed it. Eventually our spirit becomes dull and falls asleep. We become callous to the inward persuasions of the Holy Spirit.

Lust (the spirit of this world) will always put our redeemed spirit—created to respond to love (Jesus Christ)—to sleep! Our redeemed spirit was given by God to receive its nourishment from Jesus (who is love) alone. Our spirit can't feed off of lust! The world has nothing that is of interest to our spirit, so while we're partaking of the lusts of the world, our spirit sleeps. When people fall asleep in class, usually it's because they're not interested in what the teacher is teaching. As to me personally, during my school tenure there were many times when I tried with everything in me to remain awake in certain classes, but to no avail, because my instructors were so boring and uninteresting. The

Enemy puts us to sleep by making interesting to us what's uninteresting to our spirit!

So many times we leave the movies excited about what we saw, but we are sleeping. We get off Facebook and are content with all the people we connected with, but we're sleeping in the spirit. We get off the phone, excited about what we heard was going on, ready to tell someone else—but with our spirit sleeping. This is because many saints haven't heeded Paul's warning in Ephesians 5:15 to walk circumspectively. Instead of walking in the spirit, they're sleepwalking!

All things produced out of the world—movies, music, television, entertainment, views about life and marriage—are birthed out of the spirit of lust. *Our spirit is created by God to respond only to love, but all the world can feed us is lust.* It doesn't matter if the world is attempting to send out a positive message through movies, music, Internet, or any other venue of communication, or whether it is about caring, good morals, or humanitarian efforts—it is still simply lust dressed up.

The Enemy Closes Our Eyes by Opening Them

The Enemy closes our eyes by opening them! The Bible testifies that when Adam and Eve ate of the tree of the knowledge of good and evil, their eyes were opened (Gen. 3:7). The moment their eyes were opened, they died in the spirit. They died in the spirit through allowing Satan to open their eyes! As we willingly open our eyes to what is carnal, our spirit-man closes his eyes! Love can't look at lust. Love can't enjoy lust. Love can't be entertained by lust. If there is nothing else you get out of this work, if there is nothing else that you get anchored in your spirit, plunge that truth deep down in the depths of who you are in God.

When we place lust in front of love, our spirit-man closes his eyes. As we open our eyes to the movies of this world, the prime-time television of this world, the comedy of this world, and overindulgence in Facebook and the other social networks of this world, our spirit-man closes his eyes. While you are looking, your spirit will refuse to look! If anybody keeps their eyes closed long enough, they'll fall asleep. You can fall asleep in the spirit in this way as well. Many of the saints have a spirit-man with closed eyes, because their eyes and other natural senses stay open to the world too much: Eyes open to every new movie. Ears open to every conversation. Mind open to every ideology and philosophy. So often, our spirit-man's eyes remain closed because our natural man's eyes stay open too much!

The Enemy puts us to sleep in the spirit by waking us up in the natural. He works hard to make interesting to us what's uninteresting to our spirit-man, so as to put our spirit-man to sleep. The Enemy closes our eyes by opening them. If you're at every new movie premiere, if you're at every carnival, festival, and social network continuously, then more than likely your spirit is asleep! You are too open to the world to be awake unto God! "Do you not know that being the world's friend is being God's enemy? So whoever chooses to be a friend of the world takes his stand as an enemy of God" (James 4:4 AMP). You can't open your eyes to one without closing your eyes to other. Both our natural (carnal) eye and our spiritual eye can't be open at the same time! "For the flesh desires what is contrary to the Spirit, and the Spirit what is contrary to the flesh. They are in conflict with each other, so that you are not to do whatever you want" (Gal. 5:17 NIV).

Most Saints Who Are Spiritually Asleep Don't Realize It—That's Why They Remain Asleep!

Believers who are spiritually sleeping generally don't know they are asleep. They don't realize the Spirit is no longer leading them. We see this happen in the Biblical account of Sampson. Delilah was hired by the Philistines to find Samson's weakness so that they could bind him and destroy him. Once Delilah finally succeeded in convincing Sampson to tell her his weakness, look at what happened:

> Then she called, "Samson, the Philistines are upon you!" He awoke from his sleep and thought, "I'll go out as before and shake myself free." But he did not know that the Lord had left him (Judg. 16:20 NIV).

While Samson was sleeping, God's Spirit lifted off of him. He had no idea that the Spirit of God who had given him the strength to overcome in many previous battles was no longer with him, because he was asleep when the Holy Spirit lifted. There are many "Samson saints" in the body of Christ whom the Spirit of God is no longer leading but who are totally unconscious about their true spiritual condition because their spirit is asleep!

How can we recognize whether we've allowed the Enemy to put our spirit to sleep? After we leave the environment that caused God's Holy Spirit to lift like a dove, the same Holy Spirit will return. The book of Hebrews reminds us that God says, "I will never leave you, nor forsake you" (Heb. 13:5). When the Holy Spirit lifts, he doesn't leave us, he just leaves the environment that we're in, until we leave that environment. The problem is that when the Holy Spirit returns, many times he finds our spirit sleeping.

"The Holy Spirit functions to lead us into all truth" (John 16:13–14). "Those who are led by the Spirit of God, they are the sons of God" (Rom. 8:14). The Holy Spirit will come back to lead the slumberer's spirit, only to find his or her spirit sleeping. So although the Holy Spirit is leading, our spirit isn't in any condition to follow. I don't know about you, but I've never seen a sleeping man follow anybody! The Holy Spirit will begin to move us to do spiritual exercises that will lead us into the truth (Jesus Christ), or in other words, to an experience and encounter with the Living God.

The sleeping spirit can't respond to the leading of the Holy Spirit. Those that have the Holy Spirit with a sleeping spirit can sense the Holy Spirit leading them to greater levels of prayer, but because their spirit is asleep, they find that they're not able to bring themselves to pray like they know inwardly God is calling them to pray. Saints who have the Holy Spirit but whose spirit is sleeping can sense God leading them to greater study of the Word, but because their spirit is sleeping, they can't bring themselves to read like the Holy Spirit is leading them to. Every time they attempt to read and study the Word, they get nothing out of it, not because they didn't hear God's Spirit leading them to study, but because they're studying the Word with a sleeping spirit. Sleepers may be sensing God leading them to a fast, but every time they begin one, they wind up breaking it before the day is done, and they don't understand why.

As a result, many sleeping saints give up on walking in the Spirit, because every time the Holy Spirit leads them, they lack the ability to carry through. Believers with a sleeping spirit can't be led by the Spirit! We can see this in the fall of Adam and Eve. "And the eyes of them both were opened, and they knew that they were naked … And they heard the voice of the Lord God walking in the garden in the cool of the day: and Adam and his wife hid themselves from the presence of the Lord God amongst the trees of the garden" (Gen. 3:7–8). After Adam and Eve's eyes were opened, when they heard God's voice calling them—which speaks prophetically of the call of God on their lives—and they heard him walking, they ran. *God is the Spirit* (see John 4:24). When God the Spirit was walking one way, Adam and Eve were running another way! The Spirit was leading, but they weren't following! Because their eyes had been opened, they lost the ability to be led by the Spirit. Those with sleeping spirits lack the ability to be consistently led by the Spirit of God.

One might say, Since at least they have the Spirit, why does it matter why believers with a sleeping spirit give up on being led by the Spirit? "For as many as are led by the Spirit of God, they are the sons of God" (Rom. 8:14). It's not those who have the Spirit who are sons—only those who are led by the Spirit are sons of God! Sleepers can never be sons!

Why is that so detrimental to who we are in God? The letter to the Romans tells us that "if we are God's children [sons] we will receive blessings from God together with Christ" (Rom. 8:17 NCV). Also: "Everything God made is waiting with excitement for God to show his children's [sons'] glory completely" (Rom. 8:19 NCV). It's only as sons and daughters that we can experience the blessings, destiny, and purpose that the Creator created for us. Only as sons and daughters, only as those who are led, do we gain access to what belongs to us in Christ. Romans says, "If any man have not the Spirit of Christ, he is none of his" (Rom. 8:9). It's not that sleepers don't have the

Spirit of God; they do indeed belong to God. The problem is that they're not led by the Spirit they have. So they'll belong to Christ but never know what belongs to them in Christ! Upon digging even further regarding the results of having a sleeping spirit, we'll find that not waking up could eventually cost a believer more than his or her blessings, destiny, and purpose here on the earth—it could eventually cost them their eternal destiny. In the next chapter, we will look at how spiritual slumbering can ultimately cause one's name to be blotted out of the Lamb's Book of Life.

Chapter 2

Sleepers and Sinners Wind Up in the Same Boat

Being Saved and Asleep Is Just as Dangerous as Not Being Saved at All!

To be saved and sleeping is just as dangerous as not being saved at all! In the letter to the Ephesians, Paul says, "Awake thou that sleepest, and arise from the dead" (Eph. 5:14). Paul says awake, and arise from the dead; he directly connects sleep with death. This is startling, because Ephesians also characterizes the unsaved—the sinner—as being dead: "dead in trespasses and sins" (Eph. 2:1). Thus, Paul says, both the sinner and the saved sleeper can wind up in the same boat!

How can this be? If we're sleeping, it's because we're in the night. In the letter to the Thessalonians, Paul says that *they that sleep, sleep in the night*:

> But ye, brethren, are not in darkness, that that day should overtake you as a thief. Ye are all children of the light, and children of the day: for we are not of the night, nor of darkness. Therefore let us not sleep as do others; but let us watch and be sober. For they that sleep sleep in the night; and they that be drunken are drunken in the night (1 Thess. 5:4–7).

Just like the sinner lives in darkness, the sleeper sleeps in darkness. The sinner and the sleeper both live their lives in the same spiritual place.

The dark hinders the ability to see in front of you. Those who are in the dark can't know what's ahead of them. It's obvious that *both* the sinner and the sleeper live life in a way in which they don't see what's coming. They really don't see Jesus coming. They really don't see this world ending. They both live lives with their soul completely invested and tied into this current world order. Paul tells us that those saints who are sleeping really don't know where they are going for eternity. They have no true assurance and security that they will indeed enter the kingdom, just like sinners many times are unaware that their lifestyle is going to send them to hell.

Those With a Sleeping Reborn Spirit, Sin Just Like Those Who Haven't Been Reborn

Having a sleeping spirit puts you in a dangerous place. It's hard to tell the difference between someone with a reborn spirit that is sleeping and someone who hasn't been reborn at all, because both of them sin! The sinner practices sin, while the sleeper falls into sin. To be asleep is to be unconscious—unaware of what's going on in the surrounding environment. When your spirit is asleep, sin can creep. Sin can get up on you without you realizing it is there.

John 16:8 says that *the Holy Ghost will reprove, or in other words, convict the world of sin.* The Holy Spirit will warn you that sin is trying to come up on you. He'll say, "Turn that channel, it's trying to feed you lust that will birth in you fornication—sin is trying to creep up on you." The Holy Spirit will tell you, "Cut off that unhealthy friendship with that individual, you could potentially compromise your marriage—adultery is trying to creep up on you." The Holy Spirit will prompt you by saying, "Stop questioning your leader, the Enemy is attempting to place a root of bitterness in you and release rebellion and witchcraft in your ministry through you—the Spirit of Korah is attempting to come upon you." (See Heb. 12:15 and Jude v. 11.)

The problem is that while the Holy Spirit is convicting the sleeper, their spirit can't respond because it's unconscious. Remember, the sleeper has the Holy Spirit, with a sleeping spirit. The Holy Spirit is saying watch out, sin is coming. But the sleeper's spirit, the only one able to commune with him, is asleep. So the sleepers don't recognize the sin that's approaching them until it's already upon them. Like Samson, they can't see the Philistines (sin) coming; they only respond after the Philistines are upon them. "The Philistines be upon thee Samson" (Judg. 16:12, 14, 20). So instead of being awakened by the Holy Spirit, sleepers are awakened by the sin after it's bound them!

These are individuals who ask questions such as this: How did I fall like this? God, why did you allow me to do what I did or say what I said? How did I end up in such a sinful place? Sleepers will be sinners. It's not that God allowed it, but while the Holy Spirit was warning, their spirit was snoring.

Those in the Dark Can't See What's Happening, While Those in the Light Can

"Those that sleep sleep in the night" (1 Thess. 5:7). What Paul is saying is that if we are walking around with a sleeping spirit, it's because we're in the dark. When we're in the midst of true pitch-black darkness, we can't see where we're going or what's coming. A sure sign that we're sleeping is that we never see what's coming. When sleepers lose their job, they couldn't see it coming. When sleepers' marriages fall apart, they couldn't see it coming. When their children get pregnant, involved with drugs, or tied into something that could destroy their future, the parents couldn't see it coming.

Many times the trials of life come upon us unaware because we're spiritually unconscious. When we're living a life of consistent frustration and anxiety because things in the natural continue to blindside us—with no warning from the spiritual realm—it's probably a prophetic foreshadowing that we're not ready for Jesus to come. Why? Because we're never ready for anything that comes in this life. There are a lot of people in the church saying they want Jesus to come, when in fact, they're not ready at all for his second coming. If we're never ready in the natural, it's an indication that we're probably not ready for the supernatural.

To Walk in the Light Is to Have the Benefit of Seeing What's Coming

Paul says this to those of us who are awake: "But ye, brethren, are not in darkness, that that day should overtake you as a thief [with you being totally unaware]. Ye are all children of the light, and children of the day: we are not of the night, nor of darkness" (1 Thess. 5:4–5). Paul directly contrasts the sleeping saint, who is in darkness, with the consecrated saint, who walks in light. When it's light, you can do what's impossible in darkness: see where you're going, and see what's coming before it gets to you. In other words, those who are awake and live a separated life will have the benefit of receiving inward impressions of the Spirit to gain a sense of things to come, whether good or bad.

When we truly understand the hope of our calling and we truly tap into the Spirit by tapping out of this world, we have the spiritual ability to perceive what's coming before it comes. Life is not supposed to surprise us at all, because we are children of the light; we walk in the light through living a life in which we remain awake in the spirit. We'll be able to do things such as see the Enemy releasing a terminal disease against our children—and because we walk in the light and discern the attack through the Holy Spirit's warning, we can pray and fast against the sickness before it ever manifests, and our prayers will be able to turn a terminal illness into a common cold! We'll be able to face the illness by faith because we were prepared for it through the Spirit.

Examples in Scripture of Believers Who Walked in the Light

A vivid example of this in Scripture is the interaction between Paul and Agabus, the prophet.

> There came down from Judea a certain prophet, named Agabus … He took Paul's girdle, and bound his own hands and feet, and said, "Thus saith the Holy Ghost, So shall the Jews at Jerusalem bind the man that owneth this girdle, and shall deliver him into the hands of the Gentiles (Acts 21:10–11).

Agabus was walking in the light, and so he saw what was coming in Paul's life at Jerusalem. This strengthened and fortified Paul's faith to face it. Paul answered, "I am ready not to be bound only, but also to die at Jerusalem, for the name of the Lord Jesus Christ" (Acts 21:13). When we see things coming, we have the faith we need to overcome them! Only those who walk in the light are truly overcomers!

If financial famine is about to hit, because we walk in the light, we'll see it coming, and God will give us wisdom on how to invest and save money through the financial famine. We can see this in Joseph, who walked in the light. In Genesis, after Pharaoh had the two dreams about the seven healthy and ill cows, the seven healthy and ill ears of corn, Joseph interpreted the dreams—because he walked in the light, he saw what was coming in Egypt. "The next seven years will be a period of great prosperity throughout the land of Egypt. But afterward there will be seven years of famine so great that all the prosperity will be forgotten in Egypt. Famine will destroy the land. This famine will be so severe that even the memory of the good years will be erased" (Gen. 41:29–31 NLT). Joseph was able to tell Pharaoh what was coming!

Look at Pharaoh's response, because it speaks to the glory afforded to those who are awake and walk in the light of God:

> Pharaoh asked his officials, "Can we find anyone else like this man so obviously filled with the spirit of God?" Then Pharaoh said to Joseph, "Since God has revealed the meaning of the dreams to you, clearly no one else is as intelligent or wise as you are. You will be in charge of my court, and all my people will take orders from you. Only I sitting on my throne, will have a rank higher than yours ... I hereby put you in charge of the entire land of Egypt" (Gen. 41:38–41 NLT).

Joseph's light, his ability to see what was coming before it came, was his promotion! Pharaoh recognized that Joseph's ability to see was tied to the operation of the Spirit of God within him.

What God desires to pour out upon the church in these last days is the light of prophetic insight. "And it shall come to pass in the last days, saith God, I will pour out of my Spirit upon all flesh: and your sons and daughters shall prophesy ... I will pour out in those days of my Spirit; and they shall prophesy" (Acts 2:17–18). The gospel of John says that Jesus is "the true Light, who gives light to everyone, coming into the world" (John 1:9 NET). Jesus admonished his listeners in the gospel of Matthew, "Let your light so shine before men, that they may see your good works, and glorify your Father which is in heaven" (Matt. 5:16). The first letter of John says, "If we walk in the light as he is in the light, we have fellowship with one another" (1 John 1:7).

The church's glory—what is supposed to draw the world to the believer—is the light that we as believers walk in. It is our ability to tap into the spiritual realm that goes beyond that of the natural realm. People are supposed to see our light and glorify our God who gave us the light or such great insight into the things that are and that are to come.

A Last-Day Light for a Last-Day Darkness

> Arise, Jerusalem! Let your light shine for all to see. For the glory of the Lord rises to shine on you. Darkness as black as night covers all the nations of the earth, but the glory of the Lord rises and appears over you. All nations will come to your light; mighty kings will come to see your radiance (Isa. 60:1–3 NLT).

As the last days come, and as the darkness of disease, pestilence, wars, and food and financial shortages cover the earth, no one has or will have the answers for the many crucial and vital obstacles of the day. Nations and their leaders will be in the dark (see Matt. 24:6–7). God in turn is going to pour out his Spirit of light and divine insight upon the church! And not just people but nations and mighty leaders as well will flock to the church to get answers for all the darkness they face! Presidents will flock to the church to get answers for the food shortages! Military generals will form stampedes into the church to receive light, and divine insight, on how to handle military crises! Ambassadors and foreign leaders will flee to the house of God to receive light on how to handle foreign policy and negotiate foreign relations!

Jesus will pour out this last-day light for the last-day darkness the world faces! Why? Because it is God's means of bringing in the final and greatest harvest of souls right before his second coming! Mighty men, nations, and peoples will be surrendering their lives to Jesus in numbers never seen before! But probably not for the reason you might be thinking. It won't be because they're getting their needs met, it will be because they're seeing the light of the church. Nations will truly give their lives to Jesus, because they'll truly believe that Jesus is coming.

Why? They'll believe that Jesus is coming because they will see that we (the church) can accurately foresee: famine, pestilence, war, and disease coming, so when we begin prophetically declaring that Jesus is coming, masses will receive our testimony. Their faith in Jesus's coming will be fed by the light we walk in, the light to declare from our mouths so many other things that they were in the dark about.

There are two keys that I want to point out about this last-day prophetic insight that God is going to release upon the house of God. The first is that this light will be made available only to those who are willing to repent and awaken from the spiritual slumber. "Awake thou that sleepest, and arise from the dead, and Christ shall give thee light" (Eph. 5:14). We must wake up before Christ gives us light. We will examine waking up in the next chapter.

The second thing we must understand about this light is that it is not meant to be given to individuals but it is to be poured out on an entire body of believers. There are pockets of prophetic light already apparent in the body of Christ— wonderful men and women of God whom God uses to speak forth those things ordained of God, things that they saw in the Spirit before it entered the natural realm. They're able to see what's coming because they've come out of the world and have gained continuous access to the Spirit. But God's plan is to call entire congregations out (the ecclesia) and pour upon them his prophetic glory! "I would God that all the Lord's people were prophets, and that the Lord would put His Spirit upon them" (Num. 11:29).

Chapter 3

God's Wake-Up Call

Waking Is in the Shaking!

In order to walk in the light we've got to first be woken up in the spirit. In Ephesians, Paul says, "Awake thou that sleepest, and arise from the dead, and Christ shall give thee light" (Eph. 5:14). The Lord won't release to us the divine light of our inheritance until we first wake up. Since waking up is so important as we walk in our spiritual inheritance, we've got to understand how Christ wakes us up.

In the line from Ephesians shown above, Paul was quoting a passage in Isaiah that gives us the revelation of how God wakes us up in the spirit: "Awake, awake; put on thy strength, O Zion, put on thy beautiful garments ... Shake thyself from the dust" (Isa. 52:1–2). In relation to waking up, Isaiah said, "Shake thyself from the dust." When you want to wake up somebody who is in a deep sleep you've got to shake them! God wakes us up by shaking us—by allowing circumstances to shake our marriages, our health, our finances, and so forth. By these trials and tribulations the Lord attempts to shake and wake us!

God says, "Once again I will shake not only the earth but the heavens also" (Heb. 12:26 NLT). As the writer of Hebrews notes: "This means that all creation will be shaken and removed, so that only unshakable things will remain" (Heb. 12:27 NLT). God will shake the heavens and the earth in order to remove those things that can be shaken, so that only the eternal, unshakeable things can remain. The reason why nations are being shaken with financial crisis, health crisis, housing crisis, and war is because God is attempting to remove something from his people, to make it fall off or fall away. In other words we're awakened in the spirit once God removes something from us through the shaking.

Yes, God will many times allow us to go through trials that test the very core of who we are and in whom we trust, in order to bring us to the place of holiness and righteousness he has called us to. "For you, O God, tested us; you purified us like refined silver. You led us into a trap; you caused us to suffer. You allowed men to ride over our heads; we passed through fire and water, but you brought us out into a wide open place" (Ps. 66:10–12 NET). "We must go through many hardships to enter the kingdom of God" (Acts 14:22 NIV). As much as we blame all hardships, trials, setbacks, and afflictions on the Devil, in reality the very things that shake our lives are the tools that God uses to purge us and present us faultless before God.

Dust Is Thinking like Those Who Are Still in the Dirt!

Isaiah helps us understand what it is that God is going to shake off of us through allowing us to be shaken by tribulation. Isaiah says, "Shake thyself from the dust" (Isa. 52:2). When God shakes us, he's trying to shake dust off of us. What does that mean?

After we come out of the dirt (sin), we've got to deal with the dust (the mindsets, habits, perspectives, and motives) we picked up while we were in the dirt! Dust can get on you and remain on you even when you're no longer in the dirt, because dust can go airborne! There are many saints who are no longer in the dirt (sin) but they still think like those who are. They have a new heart, but they haven't taken the necessary steps to renew their mind. Ephesians says, "Be renewed in the spirit of your mind" (Eph. 4:23). God gives us a new heart, but we have to renew our minds.

It's so important to understand that having God in our hearts is not enough! We must renew our minds! "And be not conformed to this world: but be ye transformed by the renewing of your mind" (Rom. 12:2). It's by the renewing of the mind that we're transformed. It's possible to have the right heart with the wrong mind and as a result never walk in the Spirit. Ultimately, faith must be expressed through our mind, and if our mind isn't renewed, we can't walk by faith. We have to have the right mind to filter what the Spirit of God is speaking in our hearts—this is necessary so that we can ultimately walk by faith.

It is possible to have a new heart with an old mind and as a result wind up still Looking like the old man, although you have a new man living on the inside of you. How? Because the new man in us doesn't have a new mind through which to express himself. "No one can know a person's thoughts except that person's own spirit, and no one can know God's thoughts except God's own Spirit" (1 Cor. 2:11 NLT). Furthermore, "Who hath known the mind of the Lord, that he might instruct Him? But we have the mind of Christ" (1 Cor. 2:16 NLT). The Spirit of God is the mind of God. The Spirit of God's purpose is to reveal God's mind, his thoughts, to us. It is important to understand this. When the Spirit of God fills us, he doesn't fill our head, he fills our heart. The Holy Spirit is God's mind, which means God places *his* head in *our* hearts! He places his mind, his thoughts, in our hearts. God puts his mind in our hearts, and gives us the responsibility of getting it in our heads! God's mind in our heart does us no good until we get it in our mind.

So many in the church have a new life inwardly that they've never expressed outwardly, because their mind rejects and won't submit to the voice of God within them. They're in a condition in which they have the Spirit of Christ but lack the mind of Christ. They've come out of the dirt, but they are still covered in dust. The Spirit speaks to their mind, but their mind rejects it, and as a result they are never led by the Spirit.

God will go to drastic measures to shake us from the dust of carnal and worldly thinking through trials, tribulations, and suffering, even to the point of allowing bankruptcy, foreclosure, family splits, and sickness. Why?

Romans 8:14 says, "For as many as are led by the Spirit of God, they are the sons of God." Notice it does not say, As many as *have* the Spirit of God are the sons of God. Believe it or not, there are many people in the church with the Holy Spirit going to hell—because they never lived a life being led by the Holy Spirit! The Holy Spirit in our heart does us no good if we never renew our mind! He has nothing to express himself through. Sonship isn't based on simply having the Holy Spirit; sonship is based on being led by the Holy Spirit. There are a whole bunch of folks in the church who have the Holy Spirit but who aren't sons.

We must understand that we can't be led by the Spirit of Christ without cultivating the mind of Christ. So many wind up being spirit-filled, but not spirit-led, because the only way people can be led is by their head (their thoughts)! The Holy Spirit is in them, but he can't lead them, because he's the head in their heart, not head of their head. Many wind up stuck in a state in which they've come out of the dirt (sin), but are still covered in dust (the natural mind). "But the natural man receiveth not the things of the Spirit of God: for they are foolishness unto him: neither can he know them, because they are spiritually discerned" (1 Cor. 2:14).

No matter what perspective we look at it from, dust still comes from the dirt. Dust is what we have in common with those who are still in the world and under God's wrath! It's what we accrue when we spend our time outside of church indulging in and participating in the same activities as those who have no relationship with Jesus Christ!

God will shake the dust off of every true believer who has the same desires, goals, aspirations, and most importantly, thinking patterns, as those who have not subjected their lives to the Lordship of Jesus Christ. God will continue to shake the saints until he gets all of the dust off of us! He will shake us to the point at which our lifestyle as believers, and our way of thinking, in no way parallels the lifestyles and ways of thinking of those in the world.

Then and only then will the church be fully awake. Needless to say, we as the church have a long way to go before we're fully awake to who we are in God and who God is in us. Accordingly, we as the body of believers can anticipate much more shaking to prepare us for the glory of God. It's not until we're fully awake that we'll see the light of the glory of God shine upon us and be able to declare, *The works that he's done we do, and even greater works, because he is with the Father* (see John 14:12).

The good news is that once you shake someone and wake them up, there's no need to shake them anymore! God is looking for a people that "would come out from among them, and be ye separate, and touch not the unclean thing, so God can receive them" (2 Cor. 6:17), and we can receive the glory prepared for us. God wants us to wake up so that he can stop shaking and start blessing! He doesn't want to shake our finances, he wants to multiply them. He doesn't want to shake our health, he wants to release healing. He doesn't want to allow our marriages to be shaken; he wants to make them fruitful. He doesn't want to allow our employment to be shaken any longer; he wants to open doors. God is saying, "I'm ready to stop shaking and start blessing, but I want you to wake up!"

Only with Revelation Can We Rightly Divide between Good and Evil

Ephesians says, "Awake thou that sleepest … and Christ will give you light" (Eph. 4:14). Awake first, and then Christ will give you light. God won't give us light unless we're awake, unless we've shaken free of the world's dust (its way of thinking). Light doesn't just speak of prophetic foresight—light also speaks of prophetic discernment.

The creation of the world, as shown in Genesis 1:3, began by God saying, "Let there be light" (Gen. 1:3). Prophetically he was saying, *Let there be prophetic discernment.* Notice that immediately after God declared "Let there be light (Let there be discernment), he began to divide creation. God divided light and darkness. He divided the waters from the waters. He divided day and night, along with days, seasons, and years (Gen. 1:6–20)! We can't afford to miss the prophetic ramifications in that!

It wasn't until God had light that he could properly divide the creation! Only when we have light, only when we have prophetic discernment, which comes through waking up, can we truly divide, or in other words distinguish between good and evil!

As shown in the letter to the Hebrews, "But strong meat belongeth to them that are of full age, even those who by reason of use have their senses exercised to discern both good and evil" (Heb. 5:14). We can never reach our full age, we can never reach complete maturity in Christ, without waking up and receiving the light of prophetic discernment. Every time you receive strong meat, a true word from God, you should leave being able to better recognize and discern the difference between good and evil! That's one of the main purposes of the light of the gospel of Christ (2 Cor. 4:4): to give you the ability to divide, or in other words, to increase your discernment!

We as believers must understand how imperative it is that we wake up and shake ourselves from the dust and receive divine discernment. We cannot defeat the Enemy without discernment. The Enemy works hard to keep us asleep, to keep us from receiving the light of God's glory, because he understands his greatest weapon against us is deception, while our greatest weapon against him is discernment. "In whom the god (Satan) of this world hath blinded the minds of them which believe not, lest the light of the glorious gospel of Christ, who is the image of God, should shine unto them!" (2 Cor. 4:4). Satan can only bind us through deception, and we can only recognize him through discernment. As long as we're asleep, we lack the means to differentiate between Satan and God!

If We're Not Awake, We Can't Discern between Day and Night

> For such are false prophets, deceitful workers, transforming themselves into the apostles of Christ. And no marvel; for Satan himself is transformed into an angel of light. Therefore it is no great thing that his ministers also be transformed as the ministers of righteousness (2 Cor. 11:13–15).

Satan comes as an angel of light. Which means that Satan has light too! There are two lights: the light of the Gospel and the light of Lucifer! Lucifer's name means light bearer or light bringer. The Devil's counterfeit ministry comes with a measure of light. Satan actually gives us light to keep us from receiving the light of God's true gospel! There is a greater light (the light of the gospel) and a lesser counterfeit light (the light of Lucifer).

We can see this truth as God divides creation. "And God made two great lights; the greater light to rule the day [the light of the Gospel], and the lesser light [the light of Lucifer] to rule the night" (Gen. 1:16). Notice that at creation there was a light that ruled the day, which prophetically speaks of the true light of the sons of God, and a light that ruled the darkness, which speaks prophetically of Lucifer's light of deception. Paul says of the children of God, "You are children of the light, and children of the day" (1 Thess. 5:5). The true sons of God walk in the light of the day.

But there was also a lesser light given to rule the night, or in other words, a light that was of the night. Thessalonians goes onto say, "We (the children of light) are not of the night, nor of darkness" (1 Thess. 5:5). There was a lesser light from the beginning that was actually night! Satan uses this light to keep many unsuspecting saints in darkness. Many are walking in a light that actually keeps them in the dark, because there is a light in darkness. We have to be able to discern, to divide between the lesser light and the greater light of God's glory, just like God did from the beginning.

Satan Does Good Works So We'll Accept His Nature

The Devil operates under the deceptive power of the tree of the knowledge of good and evil. He presents that which is both good and evil at the same time. There is no decisive division or separation between the two in his light! Good and evil are one. That which is evil does a lot of good. Without us waking up by shaking free of the world's dust, and without Christ in turn giving us light, we will lack the ability to discern between, that which is actually evil but does a lot of good and that which is truly good.

Satan's light is true evil. One element that many are ignorant of is that true evil seeks to do a lot of good! This undetected evil that will deceive many by focusing on doing good things won't simply be the sinner seeking self-justification; Satan will seek to release most of this deceptive light right in

God's holy house of prayer. "When ye therefore shall see the abomination of desolation, spoken of by the prophet Daniel, stand in the holy place" (Matt. 24:15). Satan has well established pulpit ministries that regularly release lesser light into the body of Christ. The Devil's focus is to do a lot of good in the church so we'll accept the evil he's releasing. He'll do righteous acts so we'll accept his unrighteousness nature in God's house! Satan's ministers will feed, cloth, and school, which are good, but on the other hand, they'll also release compromise, ungodliness, and worldliness in the house of God.

Without the light of discernment, we could be actually following evil, the lesser light, and believe it is good (the greater light), because evil loves to do good, just like good does good. Sadly, I suggest to you that this is the case in much of the church body. It's the fruit of the knowledge of good and evil. We're still eating from the wrong tree because we haven't woken up. One thing we must settle in our hearts is the fact that no matter how much good anyone does, that good can never excuse their evil. True good can only be done by the righteous of God! "Every good gift and every perfect gift is from above, and comes down from the Father of lights, with whom there is no variation or shadow of turning" (James 1:17 NKJV). There is no variation, no shadow, no dark place in him or those serving in him. His light is a light with no darkness in it.

These false ministers who are of Satan, who operate in the lesser light, come across as if they're ministers of righteousness. They give you light that does good but that doesn't produce in you the true righteousness of God. They give you light on how to prosper, how to get through hard times, how to succeed in life, and how to have your best life—which in fact, is light. These uplifting messages release many benefits to the hearers, but in this life only.

The Light of the Body Depends on the Eye

The problem with these deceiving messengers is that they neglect the greater light of teaching God's people the righteousness of God. What they teach does good, but if accepted as God's good (God's light), it will keep God's people from the ultimate good (greater light). These messages and ministries, by feeding us this lesser light, will keep us from gaining the mind necessary to walk in God's eternal purposes, plans, and will for our lives. Ultimately it's only those who do God's will who shall enter into the kingdom of God (see Matt. 7:21).

Jesus said, "Your eye is a lamp that provides light for your body. When your eye is good, your whole body is filled with light. But when your eye is bad, your whole body is filled with darkness. And if the light you think you have is actually darkness, how deep (great) that darkness is!" (Matt. 6:22–23 NLT). Jesus here isn't referring to the physical body—he's speaking prophetically of the body of Christ. He's referring specifically to the way the eyes of the body either provide the body with light, if the eye is good, or release darkness into the body, if the eye is bad.

The eye of the body speaks prophetically of the visionary leadership of a particular body of believers. The eye speaks of the ministers, elders, bishops, apostles, and especially prophets of the church at large. The level of light in the body is a direct reflection of the leadership in the body. Jesus says, if the light (leadership) of the body is actually darkness, how great is that darkness. What Paul is saying is, if you are under light (leadership) that's not representing the greater light, you're actually in *greater darkness*! "If the light (leadership) you think you have is darkness, how great that darkness is!" There are a lot of people in the body who think they are receiving the greater light of the righteousness of God but are actually receiving the lesser light of worldly word and carnal consecration! So much of the church is in darkness because the Enemy is attacking the eye of the body.

The Enemy gives us a light that's in the dark, so although we're walking in a light, we remain in the dark. Being in the dark usually involves some degree of being ignorant. Satan will deceive us into remaining in a light that keeps us ignorant (in the dark) to God's radical call to sanctification and godliness.

"For they that sleep sleep in the night" (1 Thess. 5:7). The reason why there are so many believers that are asleep is because there are so many people walking in a light that actually keeps them in the night! *And those that sleep,*

sleep in the night. The light that so many saints are walking in, isn't the light of righteousness, it is a nightlight. Nightlights are only used when it's time to go to sleep. This book is a cry from God to his bride to get rid of the nightlight and wake up from her slumber!

Satan Can't Be Detected—He Must Be Discerned

Satan can't be detected; he can only be discerned by those who are awake in the spirit. There are many sleepers who, if the truth be told, are following Satan in suits and don't even know it, because good and evil are only spiritually discerned! Jesus said, "Take heed that ye be not deceived: for many shall come in my name, saying, I am [Christ]; and the time draweth near: go ye not therefore after them" (Luke 21:8). Paul says about the last days, "But evil men and seducers shall wax worse and worse, deceiving, and being deceived" (2 Tim. 3:13).

God won't give us the light to discern between ministers of righteousness and masqueraders of righteousness until we wake up! Until the body of Christ awakens from her slumber, many believers will remain in the dark.

Why is that such an alarming reality? In the gospel of John, Jesus says, "For he that walketh in darkness knoweth not where he goeth" (John 12:35). Sadly, there are many people who fill pews every week, wear Jesus T-shirts, and claim a relationship with God, who haven't the slightest clue where they're going for eternity.

In the next chapter, we'll look at the great lengths to which Jesus will go, out of his love, to wake up sleeping believers before it's too late!

Chapter 4

Jesus Is Coming like a Thief in the Night

Jesus Is Coming like a Thief to Those Who Are in the Dark

Several verses of Scripture emphasize that Jesus, when he comes, will come like a thief. "But the day of the Lord will come as a thief in the night; in which the heavens shall pass away with a great noise, and the elements shall melt with fervent heat, the earth also and the works that are therein shall be burned up" (2 Peter 3:10). Jesus warns the church of Sardis in Revelation, "Go back to what you heard and believed at first; hold to it firmly. Repent and turn to me again. If you don't wake up, I will come to you suddenly, as unexpected as a thief" (Rev. 3:3 NLT). Jesus also says, "Behold, I come as a thief" (Rev. 16:15). Paul describes the day of the Lord in First Thessalonians: "For yourselves know perfectly that the day of the Lord so cometh as a thief in the night. For when they shall say peace and safety; then sudden destruction cometh upon them … But you brethren, are not in darkness, that that day should overtake you as a thief" (1 Thess. 5:2–4).

The Scriptures make it clear that for everyone who is asleep, for those who are in darkness, the Day of the Lord—the day of Jesus's return—will be unto them as a thief. The unprepared will experience negative consequences for not being prepared for his coming. Believe it or not, Jesus comes like a thief many times throughout our lives to wake us up, out of love for us. He'll continue to do this until his ultimate coming back as a thief, at which time the condition he finds us in will have eternal consequences.

When the Bible refers to Jesus coming again, we can't just limit it to his ultimate second coming, because Jesus is always coming! Revelation 1:8 says, "Jesus is he who is, who was, and who is to come." He is the ever-coming one. He came, he's coming now, and he will come later. Jesus will come like a thief unto us now in his mercy to wake us up, so he won't have to come to us like a thief later, at his second coming, to judge us! If we're asleep, if we're walking in the dark, Jesus will come to us now, like a thief, because he is the ever-coming one.

When a thief shows up at your house, his aim is not to add something to it, but to take something away from it. And he doesn't come to steal just anything—he wants the most valuable items in the house. For Jesus to come like a thief means he's coming to take whatever we have that's valuable to us that we never gave to him. I know that this may not match your current theology, because much theology being taught today presents an unbalanced idea of God's love, one that pictures him as an "acceptor" and not a "judge." The fact is: Sleepers won't gain when Jesus comes; they'll suffer loss.

Jesus Is Coming like a Thief to Take What We Stole from Him

Jesus is coming like a thief! It's not so that he can steal anything from us, it's to take what we stole from him! Whatever we have that's valuable, that we possess, that we're connected to, that we have a desire for that's worldly, or that we're using for worldly purposes, Jesus, when he comes, will take it! Whether it's our job that we're using to fulfill the lust of our flesh, or all the stuff we purchased after feasting our eyes on it, or all the investments we made in the cares of this world, when Jesus comes, he'll take it. If the house we live in isn't sanctified and set apart for God, he'll take the house. We're in a season in which Jesus is visiting his people—not to give to us, but to take what's keeping us from him. Saints are losing their jobs, homes, families, churches, ministries, marriages, careers, children, and land. We as believers aren't simply losing these things; they're being taken from us, by God!

Whatever Is Not Consecrated Is Not Covered in Jesus's Insurance Plan

If your marriage isn't sanctified and set apart to fulfill God's purposes and plans, and you focus more on doing things together in this world than on the purpose for which God placed you together, when Jesus comes, he'll take it. Whatever you possess that's not consecrated is not covered! The coming of Christ will be a day of destruction for all those who are asleep and walk in the dark. Those walking in the light will have their jobs, homes, and marriages covered by his blood, because they will have consecrated them unto God.

Whatever we give to God we get to keep, while whatever we try to keep for ourselves Jesus will come like a thief and take. "He who loses his life shall gain it, but he who keepeth his life shall lose it" (Matt. 10:39). If it's not consecrated, it's not covered in Jesus's insurance plan! Our marriages, jobs, money—none of those are sure things unless they're consecrated unto God and his eternal purposes. Whatever we have in this life that we never truly submitted under the lordship of Christ we have no right to keep, because it's in him we live, in him we move, and in him we have our being (see Acts 17:28). We can't be in him without giving what we have to him. We get to keep what we have by making sure we give it away! If that sounds foolish to you, it's because you're attempting to comprehend it with your natural mind, not the mind of Christ.

For those who are awake, that day won't come upon them like a thief, it won't be a time of taking anything from them, because they've already given Jesus everything. Jesus will come like a thief only to those who are asleep, who are in the dark, and who haven't come to the conclusion that through Jesus, God requires complete consecration. Those who are asleep have been deceived into believing that there are parts of their lives that they themselves own. It will cost them dearly in this world so that their soul may be salvaged for the next.

Many Will Call Jesus the Thief Because He's Coming like a Thief!

Jesus takes what we have in the dark to force us to walk in the light. He takes away from us what we're enjoying in our sleep, so we can wake up. He takes what we have in the dark, so we can walk in what he's given us in the light.

We are in a season in which Jesus has come upon this nation like a thief. Many believers who go to church every Sunday have lost homes, jobs, incomes, land, businesses, families, and marriages, all because Jesus is trying to wake the body of Christ in this nation from her sleep.

The problem is that because Jesus comes upon those who are asleep like a thief, many believers mistake him for the thief! "The thief cometh to steal, kill, and destroy (John 10:10)." So many believers today fight against Jesus, who comes *like a thief*, as if he *is the thief.*

Why? Because there has been a diabolic, deceptive teaching, perpetuated by the Devil, that when anything happens that we believers don't want to happen or we deem bad, it is the Devil coming against us instead of God chastening us. This may be a news flash to you, but God chastens us much more than the Devil attacks us. Our responsibility as believers isn't so much to fight the Devil as it is to resist the Devil. The Devil attempts to get us to serve God his way instead of according to the sound Word of God. We must resist or withstand those attempts. Sadly, because many believers are biblically illiterate, they wind up serving God according to Satan's methods. When this happens, God will come in to chasten us through trial, tribulation, and the loss of things of high value to us—all to realign us and bring us back into submission to the Word of God. We resist the Devil by submitting to God. "Submit yourselves therefore to God. Resist the devil, and he will flee from you" (James 4:7). So our warfare against the Enemy isn't so much about fighting him as it is remaining in line with God.

The Antichrist Message Is about "Getting Back What Belongs to You"

Believe it or not, the antichrist spirit will be the first one preaching Go back and get your stuff! Go back and get what was taken from you. The "go back and get what the Enemy stole from you" message is one that the Devil specializes in. He wants the believers to be deceived into believing that what they're losing is a result of his attack and not God's chastisement. As a result, even as I write, many children of God have been deceived and will be deceived into fighting to take back what Jesus took from them. Satan gets the saints to fight God by making them believe that they are fighting him. Revelation 18:23 declares, "He deceived the entire world with his sorceries."

If the Enemy gets someone to fight for what they had when they were asleep, and if they get it back before they repent, they're going to go back to sleep! There are many saints that are fighting to get back things that Jesus himself took from them because they were walking in darkness! But instead of the saints allowing what we have lost in the darkness to provoke us unto the light, to provoke us unto righteousness and commitment to living the Word of God and walking in the Spirit, we remain in the darkness of lukewarm living—crying unto God to give us back what we believe the Devil has taken from us—because we've been deceived.

When sleepers are deceived into fighting to get back what Jesus took from them in time, many will lose what Jesus has given them in eternity! The Bible says that even the very elect will be deceived if it were possible (see Matt. 24:24). Saints, this isn't a time for us to go after stuff; it's a time to go after Jesus.

Sleeping Saints Are like an Un-Expectant Mother

The Bible declares of the sleeping saints, "For when they shall say, Peace and safety; then sudden destruction cometh upon them, as travail upon a woman with child; and they shall not escape" (1 Thess. 5:3). Paul likens slumbering saints to an expectant mother who knows a baby is on the way but makes no preparation to give birth. Likewise, the spiritual sleeper is one who mentally knows that Jesus is on the way but doesn't make the necessary spiritual preparation for his coming.

Paul says that although the woman is pregnant her travail comes upon her suddenly, because she doesn't properly put in place the necessary things to give birth. When it's time for the baby to come, she's not prepared. Because she is unaware, she shall not escape. The baby is still going to come, whether she's ready or not. Saints, Jesus is going to come whether we're ready or not.

To gain a revelation of what Paul is saying to us, we must think of how a pregnant woman prepares herself for a coming child, in order to understand how we as believers should spiritually prepare ourselves for the second coming of Christ. First of all, a woman who is prepared to have a child has made sure she is ready to go to the hospital. Her bag is packed and waiting. She's poised to leave for the hospital at the drop of a dime. She doesn't have to get ready—she's already ready to go.

As believers, we should have our spiritual bags packed: we should always be ready to go! Just like that packed bag is proof that the expecting mother is waiting on a baby that hasn't come yet, we as believers should have a spirit that's always ready to go and be with Jesus.

Jesus is coming back for those who walk around with the attitude of the bride, those who have a passion for him and him alone. "The Spirit and the bride say come" (Rev. 22:17 NLT). When Jesus comes back, he's going to see how many saints have their baby bag packed and ready to go. Jesus is only coming for those who are saying "Come Lord Jesus" when he comes. Those who don't have the spirit of the bride, who aren't crying out for him to come, he won't come for. We have a lot of people crying out for things in his name, but he's coming back for those who are simply crying out his name: Those who are in this world but are not of this world. Those who have their spiritual bags packed, their minds set on glory, and only one desire—to dwell in the house of the Lord (see Rev. 3:12).

Second, an expectant mother who is prepared makes sure she sets up a baby room in her house. She paints, puts down new carpet, and prepares a room that nobody else can be in but the baby, even though the baby hasn't arrived yet. When Jesus comes back, he's going to look and see if we as believers have set up a baby room for him. This baby room is place in our personal space that we've carved out just for him. Or a time of prayer and praise just for him. A time of worship and adoration in your personal space just for him. A time of study and the seeking of his face just for him. A time of service and commitment to the work of God, through the local church, just for him.

A part of not being asleep, of being awake, is having a baby room set up. It is a place in your life that nobody else can enter into, because it is reserved for Jesus, even though he hasn't come yet. It is a place where you won't allow your career, ambitions, job, hobbies, and personal agendas to intrude, because you understand that the day of the Lord will be like sudden travail upon a woman with child!

Finally, if you're sleeping, at the return of Jesus you will be in an unprepared place, just like an unprepared mother will have to give birth to her child in an unprepared place. The problem with that is she'll have to go through all the pains of labor without certain comfort measures such as an epidural. An epidural is a pain killer injected into the back of a soon-to-be mother so she doesn't have to feel all the pains of giving birth. She has to go through the birth, but she doesn't have to feel all of the pains of the birth.

If we're not sleeping, although we have to go through the same struggles that those of this world go through—employment and financial struggles, housing struggles, and all the other challenges that come with being in a nation that has backslidden and turned her back on God—we shouldn't feel all the feelings that everybody is feeling as a result of these issues, because of what God has "put in our back." We're not supposed to feel depression! We're not supposed to feel hopeless! We're not supposed to feel like we don't know if we're going to make it or not! We're not supposed to experience the same feelings those in the world experience, as the world goes through tribulation, because we're not sleeping, so we have received God's spiritual epidural in our back. We're not supposed to feel all of the pains of childbirth.

> The struggles that we're facing in the world today are the pains of childbirth. Jesus said,
>
> And you will hear of wars and threats of wars, but don't panic … Nation will go to war against nation, and kingdom against kingdom. There will be famines and earthquakes in many parts of the world. See that you be not troubled. Because all this is only the first of the birth pains, with more to come (Matt. 24:6–8 NLT).

We're not to be troubled by the birth pains of famine, pestilence, joblessness, and similar struggles, because God has given us a spiritual epidural. We've got to go through it, but we don't have to feel all the pain of it. If we're feeling all of the pain of what's going on in the world, all the emotions of those who have no faith, it's because we're probably asleep in the spirit. When Jesus comes back, he's coming back looking for those who are not focused on their feelings but are focused on their faith.

Jesus Redeems Our Eternity—We Have to Redeem Our Time!

> But the day of the Lord will come as unexpectedly as a thief. Then the heavens will pass away with a terrible noise, and the very elements themselves will disappear in fire, and the earth and everything on it will be found to deserve judgment. Since everything around us is going to be destroyed like this, what holy and godly lives you should live (2 Peter 3:10–11 NLT).

Peter raises the question, seeing that everything that is of the spirit of this world—all of its lust, all of its enjoyment, all of its good—shall be burned up: *What type of holy life should you be living?*

Paul says in Ephesians, "Walk circumspectively, walk carefully, as to redeem the time, for the days are evil" (Eph. 5:14–15). We are to live holy and separate lives, lives in which we remain awake in the spirit, because it's through holiness that we redeem the time. Even though the times are evil, we redeem the time by living set-apart lives. Jesus is responsible for redeeming our eternity; we're responsible for redeeming our time. We are called to separate ourselves from the world, because God is going to destroy everything in the world.

The problem is that many of us have had our eternity redeemed, but we're not redeeming our time. Obviously it's because we're sleeping. Something has made us unconscious of the fact that God is going to destroy everything we see. To enjoy this world is to have spiritual pajamas on. It is to pass our time indulging in what's passing away. Many sleeping saints will have on spiritual pajamas when Jesus comes back. Their pajamas will be the evidence that they were liberally enjoying what God is destroying! They won't be dressed properly before the Lord when he comes. If we're caught enjoying what God is destroying when he comes, he may have to destroy us with it!

Nobody gets dressed for work until they wake up. Until they wake up and get up, they have their pajamas on. Jesus said in Revelation, "Behold I come as a thief. Blessed is he that watcheth, and keepeth his garments, lest he walk naked [in other words, in his pajamas], and they see his shame!" (Rev. 16:15). Jesus's indictment on many when he returns is, you've done no work, and your pajamas are the proof. He'll declare, "Away from me you wicked and slothful servant, I assign you your place with the hypocrites, where there shall be weeping and gnashing of teeth" (see Matt. 25:26). This is God's earnest heart cry to his people: Wake up, for I am coming, and when I come, I'm coming quickly. May God grant us mercy and grant us a revelation of the severity of the moment.

Chapter 5

A Drunken Sleep

The Enemy Uses Intoxication to Keep the Saints from Responding to God's Word

As we have been considering one of the greatest challenges of the church today—the spirit of sleep and slumber—we've come to understand that we have an enemy that's constantly working to induce spiritual sleep upon the saints. Just like any formidable opponent, he uses more than one strategy to accomplish his agenda. The apostle Paul provides another revelation that exposes a different tactic of Satan to dull the spirits of God's people: "For they that sleep sleep in the night; and they that be drunken are drunken in the night" (1 Thess. 5:7). Paul directly correlates sleeping and drunkenness. In other words, those who are asleep in the spirit are not just asleep; they are in a drunkenness-induced spiritual sleep.

The Enemy puts massive numbers of saints to sleep by getting us drunk. You might be saying, "That can't be me, because I don't drink." This drunkenness, however, is a spiritual drunkenness. Satan is like a devious teenager who spikes the punch, mixing it with enough alcohol to cause those who drink it to be intoxicated but at the same time using enough punch to mask the taste of the liquor. We'll look at how the Enemy does this a little bit later in the chapter, but for right now it's important for us to understand how being in a drunken sleep affects us spiritually.

If you've ever had the experience of trying to wake up someone who fell asleep in a drunken state, you know that waking them up, something that should be common and simple, becomes a great challenge because of their drunkenness. You'll find that it's not like waking up a person who has simply fallen asleep. When someone is simply asleep, you can usually call their name and they'll wake up, but individuals who are in a drunken sleep won't respond to that. They usually can't be woken up by hearing a voice. No matter how many times you call their name, they lack the ability to respond because of their drunken stupor.

What's the revelation? Those who are in a sleep induced by spiritual drunkenness can't be woken up by the Word! The only way you can wake them up is if you shake them or physically move them. There are so many saints who hear the Word of God and know that Word has challenged them to repent and to change some aspect of their lifestyle, yet they won't respond to the altar call. Individuals who are in a drunken spiritual sleep have a problem with repenting!

The Word of God doesn't wake them up to their current spiritual necessity and desperate need to humble themselves before God. They'll know that God has told them to do something that they continuously put off, but they'll minimize their blatant disobedience with irreverent statements like "God is still working with me!" Their irreverent response to God's Word is proof that they are sleeping on God.

"'My hands have made both heaven and earth; they and everything in them are mine. I, the LORD, have spoken! 'I will bless those who have humble and contrite hearts, who tremble at my word!'" (Isa. 66:2 NLT). When you're spiritually awake, when God speaks, you tremble to fulfill his instruction given to you.

The Altar Is Necessary for Alterations

Individuals who are in a drunken state believe that the altar is only for sinners and not for saints. They see the altar as a place for sinners who have problems and not a place for saints who need perfection. "Therefore leaving the elementary teachings of Christ, let us go onto *perfection*" (Heb. 6:1). "And he gave some apostles; and some, prophets; and some, pastors and teachers; For the *perfecting* of the saints ... Till we come in the unity of the faith, and of the knowledge of the Son of God, unto a *perfect man*, unto the measure of the stature of the fullness of Christ" (Eph. 4:11–13).

Paul directly correlates perfection with stature. Stature comes from the Greek word *helikia* which means maturity, or of age. We can never grow into maturity in Christ without consistent, honest repentance on the altar of perfection. Accordingly, we have churches full of immature believers who haven't been to the altar since they were saved, except to seek encouragement.

These same sleeping, immature believers turn around and try to draw other people to Christ, falsely giving the others the impression that their own infantile Christian state is the crucified life that Christ calls us to. Bishops, pastors, elders, mothers, deacons, and other church leaders have gotten so drunk, and are in such a deep sleep, that they don't believe that the altar is for them anymore because of their title.

The altar is for alterations. The reason men take their suits to be altered is so that their suit will properly fit their body. The altar is necessary in every believer's life because that's where we receive the necessary alterations so that we can find our fit in the body of Christ!

Without continual alterations, we will never be able to be a properly fitting and functional part of God's body that can maintain healthy relationship with the rest of the people of God. We must continually have our perspectives, views, thinking, mentalities, and attitudes altered in order to maintain the unity of the faith, so that we can do the work of the head. Individuals who don't come to the altar will always have a hard time staying in sync with the body, because they're too haughty to ever see their own wrong.

The altar isn't just to bring alterations to us so that we can fit the body; the altar also makes us fit for our blessings, purpose, and destiny. Without the altar, we'll miss much of what God has for us.

We never outgrow the altar, no matter how long we've been walking with God. The ancient patriarchs, Abraham, Isaac, and Jacob, taught us this through their sojourning as they walked with God. No matter how long they had walked with Jehovah God, no matter how much God had used them to bring forth his divine purpose in the earth, everywhere God brought them they built an altar. No matter where we are in God, we still need alterations!

Those who are asleep reject the truth of the altar, because when suits are altered, there are portions of the fabric that have to be cut off of the suit. Being altered is uncomfortable, and people who like to sleep value comfort too much!

If We Won't Wake Up, God Will Move Us

When you wake up someone who is intoxicated, because they are in such a deep sleep, not only can't you wake them up with words but also in many cases even shaking them won't wake them up. The only way to get them from one place to another, or, the only way to get them up, is by physically picking them up and moving them. Saints who are in a drunken sleep can only be woken up when they're moved.

Because God loves his church so much, this is a season in which he is moving many saints to wake them up from a drunken sleep. Saints are having to move to other jobs, move out of their homes, and move out of churches. God is moving many of us because we're too drunk to respond to the Word alone, and if we don't respond soon, it may lead to our very destruction!

We'll see in the following chapter how the Enemy uses religious worship of Babylon to put the saints to sleep.

Chapter 6

Mixed Drinks Will Leave You Mixed Up

The Babylon Bride Is the World with Church Clothes On

The question is, How does the Enemy get so many saints to fall into a drunken sleep? I suggest to you that it ties into understanding what Babylon is and our dire need as a church to come out of Babylon. Believe it or not, many saints who are in church are still in Babylon. How could this be? Because Babylon is in the church, and the church is in Babylon. I'll explain this as we go along.

"For all the nations have drunk of the wine of the wrath of her fornication … Come out of her my people, that ye be not partakers of her sins, that you receive not of her plagues" (Rev. 18:3–4). One of the major characteristics of Babylon is that she serves the wine of fornication to those who are in her. Notice that God has to tell his people to come out of her. These are authentic believers who are drunk because they're in Babylon. What is Babylon? Babylon speaks prophetically of the false bride of Christ. Babylon is an antichrist spirit that comes in the guise of being the true bride of Christ. Notice that God refers to Babylon as "her" (a false bride).

God says that if we don't come out of "her" (Babylon, the false bride)—if we don't come out of the world with church clothes on—we will have to partake of her plagues. Everything that happens to the world will happen to us. We will lose our jobs just like the world does, when the unemployment plagues come. We will go through divorce just like the world does, when the plagues of covenant breaking sweep through the nation. Our children will suffer from the immorality of teenage pregnancy and homosexuality just like the world's teenagers do, as the plague of sexual immorality sweeps over the youth of our nation.

The people of God have accepted these spiritual plagues as the simple difficulties of life that we must all deal with, but in truth they are sufferings that the church is not called to suffer under! These plagues aren't supposed to affect us like they affect those who are outside of covenant relationship with God. We're suffering them because we're not out of Babylon and we don't realize it!

We see this truth exemplified through the releasing of the ten plagues upon Egypt during the days that the Israelites were delivered out of Egyptian bondage through the leadership of Moses. None of those plagues that affected the Egyptians touched God's people who were in Goshen. God described what would happen as he released the tenth plague, which would kill all of the firstborn in every household of those in Egypt and would lead to Israel's ultimate deliverance:

> All the firstborn sons will die in every family in Egypt … Even the firstborn of all the livestock will die. Then a loud wail will rise throughout the land of Egypt, a wail like no one has ever heard before or will ever hear again. But among the Israelites (the believers) it will be so peaceful that not even a dog will bark. Then you will know that the Lord makes a distinction between the Egyptians and the Israelites (Ex. 11:5–7 NLT).

The fact that Egypt was subject to suffer from plagues that God's people were not subject to was the distinguishing factor between the believer and non-believer. The Enemy uses Babylon to keep the true saints of God from being distinguished from those who aren't truly believers at all! He uses Babylon—the world with church clothes on—to keep us in the world, while giving us a form of godliness that suggests that we've come out of the world. He does this so that we can suffer the plagues just like the world does and there can be no true distinguishing mark between the church and the world. He does this by getting us drunk.

The Tower of Babel—A Type of Man-Made Worship

The fifty-first chapter of Jeremiah deals extensively with the religious spirit of Babylon and how God's people must come out of her. God says to his people that are in Babylon, "Come out of Babylon, my people! Run for your lives! Run from the Lord's anger" (Jer. 51:45 NCV). What we must understand is that if we're in Babylon when Jesus comes back, we'll be destroyed with Babylon! To understand how the Enemy deceives us into entering into the Babylon Bride instead of the true Bride of Christ, we've got to go back to how Babylon was established in Genesis:

> And the whole earth was of one language, and of one speech. And it came to pass, as they journeyed from the east, that they found a plain in the land of Shinar; and they dwelt there. And they said one to another … Go to, let us build us a city and a tower, *whose top* may *reach unto heaven*; and let us make us a name, lest we be scattered abroad upon the face of the whole earth (Gen. 11:1–4, emphasis added).

Babylon, the false bride, the worldly church, was established on the desire to build a city and tower that could reach unto heaven. Don't miss that, because it speaks to us of why so many saints are stuck in Babylon in a drunken sleep. The entire desire of the people of Babel was to reach heaven. The tower of Babel is a type, or symbol, of worship! The point of worship is to tap into the heavenly realm. The tower of Babel prophetically represents a form of man-made worship in which man attempts to worship and reverence God out of his own flesh instead of in the spirit.

They wanted to build a tower that could reach heaven, or they wanted to release worship that could reach heaven, but the problem was in the statement "Let us build us a tower." They were desiring to carry out the act of worship in their own strength. They were trying to worship God in their flesh. Believe it or not, the reason so many saints are asleep is because the Enemy puts us to sleep in worship! The Enemy uses a form of fleshly worship to keep us from waking up to the things of God.

We Can Reach Heaven in Our Flesh!

What happens next is what we can't miss: "And the Lord came down to see the city and the tower, which the children of men builded. And the Lord said, Behold, the people is one, and they have all one language … and now nothing will be restrained from them, which they have imagined to do" (Gen. 11:5–6). In their flesh, they were trying to build a tower that could reach unto heaven! In their flesh, they were trying to release a worship that could tap into the heavenlies. God's response to them was "Because these people are one, nothing will be restrained from them which they imagine to do" (Gen. 11:6). In other words, God was saying, "What they're seeking to do, they can actually do!" They were actually able to build a tower, or establish a form of worship in their flesh, that could reach heaven.

There is actually a level of heaven that can be accessed and experienced through our flesh, or through carnal means! Prophetically, the men at Babel were able to usher in a level of heaven and make an atmosphere conducive through worship, all without any of God's Spirit.

This means that just because we're experiencing heaven doesn't mean we're not in our flesh. Babylon is a spirit that allows you to experience a measure of heaven without coming out of your flesh—to feel a spiritual heavenly touch in a carnal state! Babylon allows you to experience the spiritual even though you aren't led by the Spirit.

This is where deception has crept into many believers' lives, because they've experienced a level of the spirit in church or in a personal time with God, and as a result they believe they are walking in the spirit. Babylon is a spirit that keeps us in our flesh through giving us a form of flesh we can experience a spirit in. Notice, I didn't say the Spirit. As long as the Enemy can keep us in our flesh, we will have to suffer the same plagues as those who are in the world.

They Were in Heaven's Presence but Not God's Presence

The Enemy has used worship to deceive so many saints into remaining in Babylon. The Bible declares that after the people had built this tower that could reach up to heaven—or in other words, after they had given worship in their flesh that tapped into the heavenlies—the Lord came down to see the city (Gen. 11:5). That is a powerful statement! But if you blink when you read it, you'll miss its implications. God had to come down to see what they had built. This means that although they were experiencing heaven's presence, they weren't experiencing the Presence of the God of heaven. If God had to come down to see it, than they hadn't reached him. They were seeing heaven in worship, but they weren't seeing God in worship.

"No flesh should glory in His presence" (1 Cor. 1:29). The Babylon Bride can bring a measure of worship in which we can experience the presence of heaven without experiencing the presence of God. As unlikely as this may sound, the Enemy keeps us out of the presence of God by using the presence of heaven! Many believers are drunk and asleep, because through deception the Enemy has caused them to mistake the presence of heaven with the presence of God.

The Enemy uses the worship of God to keep us from God. Why? Because he understands that we can never encounter God and not be transformed. He knows that the presence of God will sanctify, purify, purge, and cleanse us, and the purity we receive will lead to the fulfillment of divine purpose. "If a man therefore purge himself ... he shall be a vessel unto honor, sanctified, and meet for the master's use, and prepared unto every good work" (2 Tim. 2:21).

God said to Moses in Exodus, "No man shall see my face and live" (Ex. 33:20). When John saw the glorified Christ in Revelation, he testified, "When I saw him, I fell at his feet as dead" (Rev. 1:17). God's true Manifest Presence will always kill something in us! We can't experience his Presence and live unchanged. Something in us that is in conflict with his will, with obedience, and with total submission to him will die.

The Enemy attempts to give us an alternative form of worship that touches us without changing us! When we simply experience the presence of heaven, we can be touched yet leave unchanged.

> But who may abide the day of his coming? And who shall stand when he appeareth? For he is like a refiner's fire, and like fuller's soap. And he shall sit as a refiner and purifier of silver: and he shall purify the sons of Levi, and purge them as gold and silver, that they may offer unto the Lord an offering in righteousness (Mal. 3:2–3).

God says, "When I come, when you experience my Presence, you will experience it as refiner's fire and fuller's soap." What God is saying is that if we're going to receive God's Presence, we must receive it like soap. When someone gives us soap, we don't hold it and cry, we don't fall down in front of it, we don't tell soap all of our problems; when someone hands us soap, we wash with it. God says, "If you want Me, you want soap!" God wants us to wash in his Presence. God's Presence will wash off our lack of faith disguised as "being in a strange place." God's Presence will wash off the spirit of self-pity disguised as sensitivity. God's Presence will wash off bad attitudes disguised as "no one understands me." If we want to enter into God's rest, we can't get offended when he hands us Zest!

God's Presence is not only like fuller's soap, it is also like a refiner's fire. "God says the day of His visitation is like an oven" (Mal. 4:1). The purpose of his Presence is purging—to purify us, to remove everything in us that keeps us from giving him proper sacrifice.

We can't overlook that God says his Presence is like soap and refiner's fire. Everything that God can't wash he burns! If he can't put it in the washer, he'll put it in the oven! That's why we have to go through some fiery trials, because some stains won't come out in the washer and so they have to be burned off in the fire. God will have a church without spot or wrinkle (Eph. 5:27).

If what God is attempting to wash us of won't come clean in the spin cycle—in other words if going through the same trial over and over doesn't break us—God will be forced to burn us. "Beloved, think it not strange concerning the fiery trial which is to try you, as though some strange thing happened to you" (1 Peter 4:12).

God's Throne Isn't in Heaven, His Throne Is in the Heaven of Heavens

Babylon means confusion. Confusion means to mix or mingle two things so as to render the elements indistinguishable. Those in Babylon mix the presence of heaven with the presence of God. You might say, "Preacher, I thought you couldn't separate heaven and God, I thought to enter into heaven is to enter into the presence of God?" Not so! In Second Corinthians Paul says, "I knew a man in Christ above fourteen years ago, (whether in the body, I cannot tell; or whether out of the body, I cannot tell: God knoweth;) such as one caught up to the third heaven" (2 Cor. 12:2). There are three heavens. God's Manifest Presence, his throne, is in the third heaven.

The book of Nehemiah says, "Thou, even thou, art LORD alone; thou hast made heaven, the heaven of heavens, with all their host, the earth, and all things that are therein" (Neh. 9:6). There are heavens, but there is also a heaven of the heavens! God doesn't have his throne in the heavens—he has his throne in the heaven of heavens! He sits in the highest heaven! His Presence is found in the third heaven.

The people at Babel did tap into heaven with their carnal worship, but it was only the first heaven. Remember, God had to come down from the third heaven to see their worship. At Babel the worshippers were only experiencing the first floor. What's in the first heaven?

"For we wrestle not against flesh and blood, but against principalities, against powers, against the rulers of the darkness of this world, against spiritual wickedness in heavenly places" (Eph. 6:12). The first heaven is where spiritual wickedness dwells. The spiritual wickedness in the high heavens actually resides in the lowest heaven (first heaven). At the height of carnal worship is the lowest of spiritual beings: Satan and the demonic. Man's effort to worship God in his own strength at its best can only touch wickedness! What we must understand is that wickedness knows how to worship. Wickedness knows how to make an atmosphere conducive in a worship gathering. Wickedness knows how to usher in a heavenly environment.

That's why there are so many individuals in the church that can leave what seems to be a worship experience and carry out illicit sexual acts and other immoral activities. They can leave and still carry hate, carnality, and unforgiveness in their hearts. It's because in the midst of worship, they're not being touched by the King (fuller's soap and refiner's fire) but the demonic.

Satan uses worship to release demonic oppression upon God's people. Individuals who actually come to the service free leave bound, falling into devastating sins that destroy their families and ministries, and they never understand how in the world they got there. Many times, it's because the Enemy took advantage of them in worship!

The Enemy knows that in worship, God's people are open, and the Enemy is wicked and hateful enough to take advantage of us even in the sensitive area of worship! We think we're opening ourselves up unto God and wind up opening ourselves up to the demonic.

The Enemy Gets Us Drunk in Worship

The Enemy gets us drunk in worship. He gets us drunk with Babel, or confusion, by serving us a mix. He serves us mixed drinks to mix us up. We have times where we're experiencing the presence of heaven, while at other times we're experiencing the Presence of the God of heaven. After we drink enough mixed drinks, it becomes increasingly more difficult to discern the difference. We wind up allowing the mixed drinks to put us into a drunken sleep.

As a result, so many saints wind up spending their entire life experiencing a first heaven presence, without ever fellowshipping with a third heaven God. If God had not come down and scattered the language of those at the tower of Babel, they would have settled for a first heaven experience instead of God's third heaven Presence.

The third heaven can only be tapped into through the leading of the Third Person, the Holy Spirit. Instead we're relying on man's musical ability and gifts to bring us into the third heaven, and it alone can't. We've traded in the Third Person for practice and rehearsal. We accept the practice-sharpened sounds of praise teams and choirs, who sing demonstratively, over the demonstration of the Spirit. It's Babylon.

Chapter 7

All Worship Isn't Welcome

W e have taken note in the previous chapter that one of the Enemy's main frontal attacks on the discernment of God's people is an attack on our worship. Let's continue in that vein, and gain greater understanding of how carnal worship can destroy the discernment of God's people.

Let's examine a portion of the prophet Jeremiah's prophetic word concerning this matter. "The word that came to Jeremiah from the Lord, saying, Stand in the gate of the Lord's house, and proclaim there this word, and say, Hear the word of the Lord, all ye of Judah, that enter in at these gates to worship the Lord" (Jer. 7:1–2). God gave Jeremiah the prophetic assignment of telling Judah to repent as they entered in for worship! He was telling them to turn back to God, while they were coming to seek God. They rejected the Word of the Lord that came from Jeremiah and refused to honor his prophecies.

"Lord you are searching for honesty. You struck your people, but they paid no attention. You crushed them, but they refused to be corrected. They are determined, with faces set like stone; they have refused to repent" (Jer. 5:3 NLT). Jeremiah is saying, "You have allowed your people to be struck with sickness and disease, allowed situations and circumstances to crush them, yet they refused to see that they needed to repent—or in other words, change." This sounds like the members of twenty-first century church who blame their trials on people, or the Devil, or their haters, but refuse to ever even fathom that it's the Lord chastening them.

Much of the body has received such a lopsided teaching on grace that we don't believe that God chastens us anymore! Every affliction that comes our way, we attribute to the Devil or to people, but never to our own possible disobedience. The Bible says otherwise. "Notice how God is both kind and severe. He is severe toward those who disobeyed, but kind to you if you continue to trust in his kindness. But if you stop trusting (stop obeying), you also will be cut off" (Rom. 11:22 NLT). "My child, don't make light of the Lord's discipline, and don't give up when he corrects you. For the Lord disciplines those he loves, and he punishes each one he accepts as his child" (Heb. 12:5–6 NLT).

The reason why Judah didn't believe that they needed to return to God is because they never left the church. Their response to Jeremiah was, "How are you going to tell me to turn back to God, as I regularly come here to seek God?" In other words, how can you tell a worshipper to repent?

What Judah didn't understand is that all worship isn't welcome. The problem wasn't that Judah wasn't giving God worship, the problem was that they weren't giving God the worship he wanted. This truth is very difficult for the modern western church to embrace, but it is indeed true: all worship isn't welcomed by God.

It's hard to tell a worshipper, "Your worship needs to wash; your worship is unclean." Jeremiah was standing at the door of the temple prophesying to Judah, telling them to wash their worship. And they wouldn't receive his Word and repent, because they were regulars in worship service. The problem was that their worship was in their flesh—and only accessing the first heaven, where spiritual wickedness had access to them, as we'll see.

Praise Refused to See That She Didn't Know How to Worship!

God had a problem with Judah's worship. Judah, as we all know, means praise. God was telling the people who in type embody "praise": You don't know how to worship! Many times, the most demonstrative praisers, the ones who are always dancing, shouting, moving, and clapping while the music is playing, are the most stiff-necked and obstinate against repenting before God. They have a hard time believing that their worship is unacceptable. Their jubilant celebration of God darkens their hearts to the possibility that they're not living acceptable lives of worship through obedience unto God.

I have found that many believers in the Pentecostal movement falsely believe that their praise somehow justifies them before God. That somehow their demonstrative acts during worship service give them a stamp of righteousness before the Lord. But God was telling Judah (praise) to repent concerning its worship.

Jeremiah was declaring to the people coming to worship God that they were committing idolatry and adultery in their worship. Idolatry is the worship of other gods. Judah, or praise, knew how to honor God for what he did but didn't know how to worship God for who he was. Judah could praise God's acts but couldn't worship his Person.

Every time praise (Judah) would attempt to enter into worship, they would end up worshipping another God. Jeremiah was saying, "You're worshipping in God's house, but you're not worshipping the God of the house!" And praise refused to hear the fact that it didn't know how to worship God—that its worship was actually idolatry! I suggest to you that much of what the twenty-first century church deems worship is actually idolatry.

The definition of idolatry that I received from the Spirit of the Lord is this: Idolatry, or idol worship, is when we need something physical in order to give God spiritual worship. Idolatry is when you have to receive a physical promise to give God spiritual worship. God's problem with praise's worship was that it needed something tangible to tap into.

The issue that God has with the church today is that many praisers need an aphrodisiac in order to worship him. God is saying, "My people need an aphrodisiac in order to make love to Me." In essence, it is a form of idolatry, and it is an abominable form of worship unto God. We're feeling a touch, and we're being refreshed, not necessarily because of our love for God, but because of the toy that we're requiring God to give us in order to get us in the mood to worship him. We respond in worship because we're told about the "open door," "the blessing," or the "great season" that we're about to walk into. All of these have their place, but God has called us as a people to worship him in spirit and truth, not in presents and promises.

An aphrodisiac is defined as an agent that acts on the mind and causes the arousal of the mood of intimate desire. An aphrodisiac is actually exotic foods that are supposed to get you in the mood for intimate relationship. What God is saying to the church today is, "In your worship services, you're requiring certain foods to get you in the mood! Certain words in order to get you going. You've got to be told that I'm going to bless you. You've got to be told how your praise is giving you a breakthrough. You've got to play certain music and get a worship leader in front of you, and he or she must say all the right things to get you in the mood to make love to (worship) Me!"

God is saying, "I've got a problem with that!" What the use of a spiritual aphrodisiac indicates is that a believer thinks, "I need something besides you, God, to get me in the mood to make love to you! You, all by yourself, are not enough to get me in the mood to worship." In other words, it's not just about the worshipper and God; it's about the worshipper, God, and it! Many of us are not in the mood for God without it.

There are saints that can come into church who will sit with their legs crossed and arms folded the entire time of worship, if the church doesn't get the aphrodisiac right—if the praise team doesn't sing their song. Or if the presider doesn't excite them with catchy phrases, many people won't budge. Aphrodisiacs are an abomination unto God! They're detestable, and they literally make God sick. When God sees an aphrodisiac in the worship bed, he'll refuse to get in it.

Sadly, because of the mass numbers of carnal people filling the pews of our churches, the church leaders are focusing on giving a natural thrill to people who lack a spiritual hunger and thirst. Many servants of Satan have risen up to feed churchgoers flesh—instead of the bread that comes down from heaven—and to regularly use other things rather than God to get their congregations to worship him. Through spiritual aphrodisiacs, so many are baited into believing they're worshipping Jehovah God when in fact they are worshipping their own aspirations, dreams, goals, feelings, and belly.

The term aphrodisiac comes from the name of the Greek goddess of love, Aphrodite. So when we need a spiritual aphrodisiac to worship God, we're actually worshipping the Greek goddess, Aphrodite. We're committing idolatry. Idolatry opens us up to the demonic!

We Commit Adultery When We Commit Idolatry

Idolatry and adultery are closely related. When we commit idolatry in worship, we also commit adultery. Let me explain. Starting from the understanding that worship is intimacy with God: if God won't get in our bed when we have an idol in it, we must ask, What *is* getting in our worship bed? I know people are actually being touched by something while the music is playing, because people are falling out, dancing, shouting, crying, and lifting up their hands.

I suggest to you that there are times in which we commit adultery on God in worship and we don't know it!

God is a spirit, and they that worship him must worship him in spirit and truth. We commit adultery on God in worship when we open ourselves up and allow another spirit besides the spirit of God to touch us in worship! Second Corinthians says, "If one comes and preaches another Jesus besides the Jesus we (the apostles) have preached, you'll receive a different spirit" (2 Cor. 11:4). If we receive another word, we'll be touched by another spirit.

A person knows if they're committing adultery on their spouse, they know if they're sleeping with someone else outside the marriage, but how do we know if we're sleeping with another spirit? How can another spirit get into our worship bed? How does the Enemy get us to accept "first heaven" worship and to open ourselves up to spirits that touch us but don't change us?

Judah in the Valley Is like a Female Donkey in Heat!

> You are like a wild female donkey brought up in the wilderness. In her lust, she sniffs the wind to get the scent of a male. No one can hold her back when she is in heat (This is about intimacy, worship). None of the males need wear themselves out chasing her. At mating time she is easy to find (Jer. 2:24 NET author's emphasis).

In verse 23, Jeremiah prefaces this statement with "See thy way in the valley," or in other words, "See how you act in the valley."

He's talking prophetically about how the believer begins behaving when going through valley seasons in his or her life. When life is hard and we're struggling. When we're waiting on God and he's not coming. When everything is working against us and nothing is working for us. In effect, Jeremiah says to the people about the valley seasons, "You are like a female wild ass during mating season!" (See Jer. 2:24.) Jeremiah compares the people of God in their valley season to a female donkey that is in estrus or "heat."

A female donkey goes into heat during the spring or early summer. The female donkey is in heat for only two to seven days. Because she has only these few days to get pregnant, she'll open herself to any male donkey that's available during that window of time. If you don't mind me personifying this simile given by the Holy Spirit: The male donkeys don't have to take her on a date. They don't have to promise her a house; they don't even have to have a job. All they have to do is show interest, and she'll let them in.

God is saying that the saints are like that when we're in our valley seasons. We act in our spiritual life like a female donkey acts in heat, willing to open ourselves up to any spirit that has anything good to say about us! When we're in the valley, when we're going through financial difficulties, employment issues, mental and psychological strain, and various other trials and tribulations, we'll open ourselves up to any spirit that will tell us things are about to get better, any spirit that will declare that God is about to open doors for us, that God is about to vindicate us.

Jesus may be nowhere in the room or in the word that's being preached, but we'll open ourselves up, because we're in heat! God may be refining us, rebuking us, correcting us, or afflicting us to bring us unto repentance and closer to the image of Christ, but we'll miss our refining. Babylonian worship never focuses on what God wants to do *in* us but only on what God wants to do *for* us. So we're blinded to the reality that what's going on around us may have been set up by God to deal with something in us. The Bible does say that it is through many afflictions that we enter into the kingdom of God (see Acts 14:22).

The Church Is Being Raped Instead of Refined

When a female donkey is in heat, she gives off a scent that lets all the male donkeys in her vicinity know that she's open. Male donkeys can smell a female donkey in heat, and they are drawn by that smell, gathering around her to get their opportunity for intimacy with her.

As it is in the natural, so it is in the spirit. When spirits see the saints in heat, they line themselves up to have intimacy with us (worship), just like male donkeys line up to have intimacy with a female donkey in heat! They know it's their opportunity to come in. False teachers and false prophets thrive in seasons in which the saints of God are in heat—by preaching another gospel, releasing another spirit, and taking the focus off of Christ and the righteousness he's called us to. So the spirit of lust is preached in a package with love's name on it. Walking by sight is preached in a package that reads walking by faith. Happiness preached in a package with holiness written on it. Pleasure is preached under the guise of purpose. Self is hidden in the package of self-denial. Remember, if we receive another gospel, we also receive another spirit (Gal. 1:6). When we're in heat, the Enemy comes as an angel of light to pervert our inner-man and render us unable to discern between good and evil.

The reason why God can't get pure worship out of the church is because the church is used to being with a multiplicity of spirits. Without realizing it, we're accustomed not to one spirit in worship, but many. So when it's time to just stand up, lift up our hands, and worship God for one single reason—because of who he is—we find it challenging, because we're so used to having so many spirits to help get us in the mood. There is the music, the drums, the presentation of praise. We find it hard to worship one spirit when we've been intimate with so many other spirits. Spiritual adultery has made it difficult for God's people to walk in spiritual fidelity.

Judah Committed Idolatry and Adultery in High Times

God says to Judah in the book of Jeremiah, "When upon every high hill and under every green tree thou wanderest, playing the harlot" (Jer. 2:20). Also, "Look up at the hilltops and consider this. You have had sex with other gods on every one of them" (Jer. 3:2 NET). The prophet also said, "The Lord says … Hast thou seen that which backsliding Israel hath done? She is gone up on every high mountain and under every green tree, and there hath played the harlot" (Jer. 3:6). It was further said, "Our worship of idols on the hills and our religious orgies on the mountains are a delusion. Only in the Lord our God will Israel ever find salvation!" (Jer. 3:23 NET).

One thing we can't overlook is that Judah committed her idolatry and adultery in high places. On the hills and the mountains. High places prophetically speak of high praise. Having a high time in God. A time when the spirit is high in the house. Judah's problem was the hills and the mountains. They would always commit adultery when the spirit was high. The times in which we commit adultery the most, when many unclean spirits enter into the house, is when we're having a high time in God!

Why? Because when the spirit is high, we take for granted that God's spirit is the only one making it high! When we're in a low valley, and we enter into a high praise, we take for granted that everything that we experience on the hill is God. So we wind up committing adultery on every high hill. We forget that Satan usually shows up for worship. "Now there was a day when the sons of God came to present themselves before the Lord, and Satan also came among them" (Job 1:6 ESV).

The church has gotten to the place where we begin to believe that we have to have a high time in order to experience God's delivering power. We come to church only looking for a high time, and we open ourselves up to spiritual wickedness in high places.

God Wants to Teach Us That He Doesn't Need a Hill to Deliver Us

In Jeremiah it is stated, "Truly in vain is salvation (deliverance) hoped for from the hills, and from the multitude of mountains; truly in the Lord our God is the salvation (deliverance) of Israel" (Jer. 3:23). Salvation—deliverance—isn't necessarily found in having a good time; salvation is found in submitting to a good God! Salvation is found in repentance, obedience, and submission. Sometimes submitting to a good God may not mean having a good time, but it will bring us into deliverance.

In the next chapter, we'll look more closely at the Babylon Bride so that we can discern this false system of worship and come out of her!

Chapter 8

The Music Is Magic

Babylonian Worship Emphasizes What You Do When the Music Is Playing

B abylon intoxicates the people of God in worship because she is musically gifted. Babylon puts a lot of emphasis and passion in her musical sound, as does the Bride of Christ. Babylon has a profound sound that inspires individuals in worship and praise, that's why it's so hard for us to come out of her, because she sounds so good! The false bride's music has a hypnotic effect. No wonder, because Satan himself was the worship leader in heaven. We can see the revelation behind the captivating sound of Babylon through the writings of the prophet Daniel while God's people were under Babylonian captivity:

> Neb-u-chad-nez'zar the king made an image of gold, whose height was three score cubits, and the breadth there of six cubits: he set it up in the plain of Du'ra in the province of Babylon … Then an herald cried aloud, To you it is commanded, O people, nations, and languages, That at what time ye hear the sound of the cornet, flute, harp, sackbut, psaltry, dulcimer, *and all kinds of musick, ye fall down and worship the golden image* that Neb-u-chad-nez'zar the king hath set up (Dan. 3:1–7, emphasis added).

Notice that the worship that was established by the Babylonian empire hinged on the playing of music. Only when the cornet, flute, harp, sackbut, psaltry, dulcimer, and all kinds of music began to play would everyone fall down and worship.

Everyone was to worship the image that was set up by the king. Babylonian worship is an image, an idol, that can't go forth without music. It is a worship system set up by man, one that uses music to bring believers into a form of worship that doesn't have God as its focus and center.

Babylonian worship focuses on what you do while the music is playing. As long as you're worshipping when the music is playing, you're considered a worshipper! It doesn't matter what you do before the music starts, or how you live after the music stops—you're considered a worshipper as long as you bow when the music is playing. It's a system of worship that doesn't demand sanctification, denial of self, and living a life focused on completing God's will.

True worship focuses on the way you live when the music stops. In Daniel, the king's edict was that whoever refused to worship while the music was playing would be thrown in a fiery furnace. (See Dan. 3:6–7). In other words, if you don't praise God while the worship is going *forth*, you're going to go *through*. Sound familiar? Doesn't much of the Pentecostal ideology tell us that if we don't dance we won't get our breakthrough? That if we don't worship while the music is playing, our life won't change. That because we don't bow when the music is playing, we'll miss God! We'll be thrown in the furnace for it.

Have you ever heard any of those statements in worship service? Have you ever been told that you'll be thrown in the fire for what you're not willing to do while the music is playing? It's a direct manifestation of the Babylonian spirit. Babylonian worship tells you that what's hindering God from moving in your life is what you're not doing while the music is playing, never even considering sin, iniquity, carnality, or the need to repent as possible reasons why you're going through what you're going through. This worship never truly emphasizes the necessary inward change that God demands of all those he would deem sons.

Babylonian worship focuses more on the dance you do while the music is playing than on your inability, when the music stops, to forgive folks who have hurt you. Babylonian worship focuses more on the praise you give God while the music is playing than on the sacrificial life you give him when the music stops.

God says in Jeremiah, "Your iniquities have deprived you of wonderful blessings, and your sin has robbed you of many good things" (Jer. 5:25). Here, God didn't mention what you do or don't do when the music is playing. It's not that I'm saying that we shouldn't bless God through dance, the lifting of our hands, shouting, and standing. But all of that is just one factor of true worship. True worship is a lifestyle that is given over to God beyond the borders of music, and more so through obedience unto God, even through suffering.

We Focus on Our Moves Instead of on God Moving

Notice the fact that Babylonian worship was activated and inspired by fear. All those who refused to worship while the music was playing would be thrown in the fire. The Enemy gets us to worship an image through fear instead of faith. We worship God out of a spirit of manipulation instead of adoration. We worship him while the music is playing because we don't want to be thrown into the fire, we don't want to miss our blessing or our breakthrough.

The problem is that fear doesn't move God, faith does! The Enemy gets us to worship an image through fear! As a result, we wind up doing a lot of dancing, a lot of movement in church, but not seeing God move when we leave. So church becomes more about us moving than God moving! When people begin to break out in high praise, and everyone is dancing, we equate that to God moving. It becomes all about our praise instead of all about our Promisor! Worship becomes man-centered instead of God-centered.

Our Music Can Ascend to Heaven Even When We're Not Going to Heaven

The reason why it's so hard to come out of Babylon is because those in Babylon are musically gifted. They're carnal believers who haven't come out of the world, but their music can bring you into the heavens. Many times, we as believers make the mistake of thinking this: Because you can take me up to the heavens with your music ministry, you must be living a set-apart life. Babylonian musicians live lifestyles that are still of the world, but their music ascends unto heaven. Since their music ascends unto heaven, we accept their lifestyle as heavenly. So when they play music, we bow to their idol. We bow to the god they worship, one that doesn't require them to come out of the world before they can truly worship God.

Our call of coming out of the world is paralleled in Scripture to God's call to bring the children of Israel out of Egypt. God said to Pharaoh through the mouth of Moses, "Let my people go, let them come out of Egypt, so they can worship me in the wilderness!" (Ex. 8:8). God made it clear that Israel couldn't worship him until they came all the way out of Egypt. We must come completely out of the world before we can truly worship God. Babylonian worship has the ability to give you an experience of heaven although you're not truly out of the world. Their musicians can help you experience a measure of heaven, even though they themselves aren't heavenly! As a result, the people of God fall asleep! We wind up accepting their lifestyle along with their music as worship, when in fact it isn't.

Witchcraft Worship

Babylon, the world with church clothes on, keeps the saints asleep and worldly through her music! As we look at Babylon in the Book of Revelation, you'll see that same consistent factor, which is that Babylon's dominion comes through a false, carnal, worship, through the hands of skillful musicians:

> And a mighty angel took up a stone like a great millstone, and cast it into the sea, saying, Thus with violence shall that great city Babylon be thrown down, and shall be found no more at all. And the voice of harpers, and musicians, and of pipers, and trumpeters, shall be heard no more at all in thee ... for thy merchants were the great men of the earth; for by thy sorceries were all nations deceived (Rev. 18:21–23).

The first thing that will be destroyed in Babylon, the Bible declares, is her music! Why is music the first thing that will be destroyed? Babylon doesn't merely deceive the church; it's a spirit that deceives the nations.

How in the world can music deceive the nations? It's because the Bible doesn't just refer to it as music, but sorcery. Verse 23 says that "by thy sorceries, the nations were deceived." Sorcery is witchcraft, magic and spells. The reason why this music will deceive so many is because it's not worship—it's witchcraft.

The music is actually a form of magic. Magic is defined as the art of producing illusions. An illusion is something that appears to be real, but in actuality it's not. Babylonian music produces an illusion of worship!

Sorcery makes you feel like your worship experience is real when in actuality it may not be. Music that's magic, will allow you to experience the presence of heaven in your flesh. It won't require you to change anything to experience heaven, all you have to do, is bow when you hear the music. It brings you into the first heaven, where spiritual wickedness abides, but doesn't tap you into the third heaven, where God's Presence abides (see chapter 6).

That's why many individuals under the influence of witchcraft worship, only truly experience liberty when the music is playing! In other times they are bound by sin, iniquity, addictions, and heaviness. Their worship gives wickedness access to their lives, and as a result, they live the majority of their lives defeated, confined to experiencing liberty only when the music is playing.

God Will Have Your Back When You Have His!

> The Lord hath made bare his holy arm in the eyes of all the nations; and all the ends of the earth shall see the salvation of our God. Depart ye, depart ye, go ye out from thence, touch no unclean thing; go ye out from the midst of her; be ye clean, that bear the vessels of the Lord [the believer] (Isa. 52:10–11).

In the New Century Version, verse 12 of Isaiah 52 says, "You will not be forced to leave Babylon quickly; you will not be forced to run away, because the Lord will go before you, and the God of Israel will guard your behind."

God tells his people to go out of her. He will not force us to leave Babylon.

God will only go before us. In other words, he'll lead us out, but he won't force us out. We have to choose.

The Bible declares that if we follow him out, his glory will be our rearguard. He'll only get behind us after we get behind him. He doesn't have our back until we have his back. "For the Lord goes before you; the God of Israel is your rearguard" (Isa. 52:12 NET). He'll guard our back.

The back is our blind spot. It's the place where something can come upon us without us knowing it. If we wake up, however, nothing will be able to catch us off guard. In God's glory we have the spiritual ability to know what's coming before it comes. It is the prophetic light that God promises to those who wake up, mentioned in chapter 3 of this book. What God is saying prophetically is, "If you wake up, nothing will be able to come upon you unaware! I'll have your back, or your blind spot!" But the Lord won't have our back until we come out of Babylon. God's declaration is, "Come out of compromising worship, and worship me in spirit and in truth" (see John 4:23).

Sleep Will Eventually Become Death

God says that if you don't come out of Babylon, the result will eventually be a spiritual sleep that you'll never be able to wake up from, and you'll miss the kingdom—sadly doing the most unlikely thing: worshipping.

> While they are stirred up, I will give a feast for them and make them drunk. They will shout and laugh. And they will sleep forever and never wake up! Says the Lord" (Jer. 51:39 NCV). I will make Babylon's rulers and wise men drunk, and her governors, officers, and soldiers, too. Then they will sleep forever and never wake up, says the King, whose name is the Lord All-Powerful (Jer. 51:57 NCV).

God says that all of Babylon's leaders will sleep. That means they don't even qualify to wake God's people up. They can't give you a word—all they can do is read you a bedtime story!

CHAPTER 9

WHAT'S BEHIND YOUR WORSHIP?

Son of man, take up a lamentation upon the king of Tyrus, and say unto him, Thus saith the Lord God; Thou sealest up the sum, full of wisdom, and perfect in beauty. Thou hast been in Eden the garden of God; every precious stone was thy covering, the sardius, topaz, and the diamond, the beryl, the onyx, and the jasper, the sapphire, the emerald, and the carbuncle, and gold: the workmanship of thy tabrets and of thy pipes was prepared in thee in the day that thou wast created (Ezek. 28:12–14).

Satan Was Jesus's Armor Bearer

Isaiah is prophetically describing the Devil before his fall. He's describing Lucifer as the light bearer, the Morningstar, the anointed cherub that covered. That reference to Lucifer being anointed to cover indicates to us the nature of Satan's relationship with Jesus in ministry: he covered Jesus in ministry. In a sense, he was the Lord's armor bearer. He and the Lord had a close-knit relationship.

He was also the Morningstar. The morning star is the light that you see right before the sun's presence comes out. Satan was Jesus's morning star; his presence would always immediately precede the very presence of the Lamb! Lucifer was so anointed by Jesus, he was so charismatic, that every time you experienced his presence, you knew that you were about to experience the presence of the Lord. Every time he came out, you knew Jesus was about to come out. His presence was an indication that God's presence was right around the corner. He was anointed to usher in the anointed one. Every time you got close to Lucifer's presence, you began to sense and experience the very Presence of Almighty God.

How was Lucifer's presence so correlated with the Presence of God? The Bible says, "The workmanship of thy tabrets and of thy pipes was prepared in thee in the day that thou wast created" (Ezek. 28:13). Satan was created with the worship instruments built inside of him. He didn't play the organ—he was the organ. He didn't play the drums—he was the drums. He didn't play the bass—he was the bass. He didn't give worship—he was worship! He was heaven's music! He was heaven's worship leader. Heaven didn't have worship service without him.

Now how did that lead to Satan ultimately being filled with pride and being excommunicated from the heavenly Jerusalem? Here's how. Heaven is the place of perpetual worship. Worship must be constant and consistent in heaven, because God's Manifest Presence is always on display. Because worship is always necessary, Lucifer was always necessary. Lucifer was always needed.

The Worship Was So Powerful Because It Was So Close to The Word

Because Lucifer was so close to God, as the angels heard the music from the chief musician they would begin to lift up their hands. They would begin to cry. They would lie down prostrate on the floor. They would cry out "Holy, holy, holy." They would respond this way because of the worship flowing from the worship leader. All this would take place just through Satan's ministry, preceding the presentation of the Presence of the Lord.

This worship, as it does today, would cause the angels to be open in their spirit to whatever God desired to do or say. But although the angels experienced much through Satan's music ministry, they hadn't experienced the Lamb (the Word) yet.

After Lucifer's ministry would come The Word (Jesus Christ); The Word would come behind the worship to release glory on the angels while they were open through worship. The Word would come behind worship and release his power and glory upon them while they were open through the worship.

Through the heavenly pattern, we can see the true order, protocol, and relationship between worship and the Word. Worship is supposed to open us up so that the Word can come in and impregnate us with the things of God. Worship and the Word (Jesus Christ) are not to be divorced from one another. Music/worship was created for the Word, and the Word isn't supposed to go forth without worship. The only reason why the worship operated in the anointing it operated in is because it was so close to the Word. Satan's assignment as the chief musician was to prepare the way for the Lord.

Satan Deceived the Angels with Worship

Satan began thinking this: "Every time the angels come into my presence, they begin crying out, lying prostrate, and worshipping, and I wind up having to step aside and allow them to worship him (Jesus), but they began worshipping when they experienced my music ministry. So they might as well worship me."

The Bible testifies, in Revelation 12:4, that Satan convinced a third of the angels in heaven to worship him. How did he do that?

Through worship, Satan deceived the angels into minimizing worship to the music alone. Satan began holding worship events without the Word. And the same things happened at his events as did when he was covering Jesus. As Satan played, the angels would lift their hands, they would cry, they would lie prostrate on the floor, but there was no Word (Jesus) behind it.

So the angels were deceived by the music that captured their emotions and released in them a desire to worship; But what they were getting through Lucifer's ministry wasn't in itself a God experience. Lucifer entrapped angels into focusing more on the music (worship) than the Word (Jesus Christ). They didn't realize it, but they weren't worshipping God, they were worshipping music. They were worshipping a sound. They were worshipping worship! They were worshipping Satan!

Every Musician Will Be Tempted to Get Men to Worship Them

Musicians, including worship leaders, will always be tempted with the sin of the original worship leader: to get people to worship them instead of God. Of course, every musician's immediate response to that statement is, "I would never play music for people to worship me!" But if you're attempting to lead worship without the Word, if you're a musician in the church and you're not living the Word, those who respond to your music are worshipping you, because you don't belong to Jesus.

Those who don't belong to God can't lead worship unto God, because they themselves aren't worshipping God. You can always tell when worship leaders are operating in this spirit, because there will be an overemphasis on the music and musicians and a de-emphasis on the Word and God's will. There will be an emphasis on an atmosphere of group participation and a de-emphasis on the altar that demands us to die to ourselves. It will be more about entertainment than edification.

Music's purpose from the beginning was to always precede the Word, to prepare the Word's way. If there was no Word behind the music, there was no point for the music. Thus, today, if the music being played isn't inspired by God, if it's not inspired by the Word, then it has no place in a worship leader's life. All worship leaders will be tempted to play music outside of its purpose, which is to glorify God. Today's musicians will be constantly tempted to play in clubs, to play for secular artists, to sing in bars, all with the justification of making ends meet. It's a trick of the Enemy to pollute and pervert worship in the church.

The Enemy Is Deceiving Many Musicians into Disqualifying Themselves

Satan's agenda is to get those that carry the burden of worship in the church to disqualify themselves from operating in the level of music ministry that can usher in the true Presence of Almighty God. Their singing may emotionally exhilarate people, bringing them to tears, inspiring them to dance and lift their hands, but it won't carry the necessary level of anointing, which places a demand on the worshippers to continue to be conformed into the image of Christ.

How does Satan do this? By getting musicians to play music for purposes outside of kingdom purposes. If you're a musician who's willing to play music outside of the Word, your music won't carry the anointing to open people's hearts to the Word! You can't play for the church and for the world. The Enemy is deceiving many anointed vessels into disqualifying themselves from their music ministry, because *no man can serve two masters*! (See Matt. 6:24.)

God is looking for worship leaders in this season that are willing to serve only him. Some musicians are willing to play for pay in the world and then turn around and attempt to play for purpose in the church. What is actually taking place is that anointed musicians are trading purpose for pay! Please hear the Word of the Lord, hear God's call for spiritual fidelity, and repent! "Therefore now amend your ways and your doings, and obey the voice of the Lord your God; and the Lord will repent him of the evil that he hath pronounced against you" (Jer. 26:13).

The Playing of Music in the Church Is a Redemptive Act

Playing instruments is a redemptive act within itself. We can never forget where all instruments originated: they were created in Satan's body. When a musician is holding an instrument, they are literally holding a part of Satan's body!

Musicians are literally assigned to use Satan's body as one of the main tools to build the body of Christ. God uses musicians to play the Devil! If you're truly an anointed and faithful musician, every week, you're not just playing—you're playing the Devil. That's why those in the music and arts department are always under constant attack. Sexual immorality, compromise, and carnality are always attacking those who operate in the music ministry. Satan will never leave musicians alone, because the instrument they're using is a part of his body. He knows that his body plays a key role in bringing individuals back under the Word of God.

Ultimately, Satan wants his body back. Satan's kingdom—in every way, shape, and form—is a counterfeit to God's true kingdom. "Wherefore when he [Jesus] cometh into the world, he saith, Sacrifice and offering thou wouldest not, but a body hast thou prepared for me … Then said I, Lo, I [Jesus] come (in the volume of the book it is written of me,) to do thy will, O God" (Heb. 10:5, 7). Satan is seeking a body to do his will just like God is.

That's why Satan attacks the music ministry relentlessly. If he can get the worship leaders to fall into sexual sin, he can get his body back. If he can get the praise team members to begin compromising God's moral pillars, he can get his body back. If he can tempt those who are assigned to usher in God's Presence to begin ministering out of personal ambition more than simply for God's glory, he can get his body back. As musicians, your responsibility to walk upright and blameless before the Lord is of the utmost importance, because you can't afford to fall into sin and give Satan his body back.

Instruments Came from Cain's Line

> And Cain went out from the presence of the Lord, and dwelt in the land of Nod, on the east of Eden. And Cain knew his wife; and she conceived, and bare Enoch: and he builded a city, and called the name of the city, after the name of his son Enoch. And unto Enoch was born Irad: and Irad begat Mehujael: and Mehujael begat Methusael: and Methusael begat Lamech. And Lamech took unto him two wives: the name of the one Adah, and the name of the other Zillah. And Adah bare Jabel: he was the father of such as dwell in tents, and of such as have cattle. And his brother's name was Jubal: he was the father of all such as handle the harp and the organ (Gen. 4:16–21).

The Bible declares that Jubal, who was a descendant of Cain, was the father of all who handled, or played, the harp and the organ. Jubal is widely associated by most theologians and historians with the invention of musical instruments. So music was birthed out of Cain's line. Cain's line invented musical instruments, because musical instruments came out of Satan's body.

I suggest to you that Cain's father wasn't Adam, it was Satan! "How can you say that, preacher? What did Cain do?" He killed his brother Abel in Genesis. He killed his brother at the beginning (Genesis). Jesus said to the Pharisees, "You are of your father the devil, and the lusts of your father you will do. He was a murderer *from the beginning*, and abode not in the truth, because there is no truth in him. When he speaketh a lie, he speaketh of his own: for he is a liar, and the father of it" (John 8:44, emphasis added).

Jesus told the religious leaders, the Devil is your father because you want to kill me, and the fact that you want to kill me is proof that you came from the loins of a killer. Jesus states a principle here that we can't afford to miss. He was saying that those who kill come from the loins of killers. Cain killed Abel, so his father was a killer! I suggest to you that there was more that happened between Eve and the serpent than just eating a piece of fruit. She was impregnated with Satan's seed (Cain). The Bible makes it clear in Genesis that "the serpent was more subtle, crafty, and clever than any living creature of the field which the Lord God had made" (Gen. 3:1). Adam and Eve were naked when the serpent came with his temptation. I won't go any further with that, but it's certainly something to ponder and pray about.

CHAPTER 10

DON'T LOSE THE HEAD IN YOUR DANCE

At that time Herod the tetrarch heard of the fame of Jesus, And said unto his servants, This is John the Baptist; he is risen from the dead; and therefore mighty works do shew forth themselves in him. For Herod had laid hold on John, and bound him, and put him in prison for Herodias' sake, his brother Phillip's wife. For John said unto him, It is not lawful for thee to have her ... But when Herod's birthday was kept, the daughter of Herodias danced before them, pleased Herod. Whereupon he promised with an oath to give her whatsoever she would ask. And she, being instructed of her mother, said, Give me here John Baptist's head in a charger ... and he sent, and beheaded John in the prison (Matt. 14:1–10).

And in those days Peter stood up in the midst of the disciples, and said, (the number of names together were about an hundred and twenty,) Men and brethren, this scripture must needs be fulfilled, which the Holy Ghost by the mouth of David spake before concerning Judas, which was guide to them which took Jesus. For he was numbered with us, and had obtained part of this ministry. Now this man purchased a field with the reward of iniquity; falling headlong, he burst ascunder in the midst, and all his bowels gushed out (Acts 1:15–18).

Herod Traded In John's Head for a Dance

Herod was king of Judea, a man of power, influence, and prestige, yet John was publicly preaching against his sin, declaring, "Herod, it is not lawful for you to have Herodias, your brother Phillip's wife!" The Bible says that Herod, out of a desire to maintain his reputation and authority, had John placed in prison for preaching against his trespass.

Although Herod had thrown John into prison, he respected him, so he wouldn't kill him. But he had a birthday party, and Herodias's daughter danced for him at this celebration. He was so pleased by the dancing that he told her, "I'll give you anything you ask for in return for your dance." The Bible declares that she asked for John's head on a plate.

Because Herod didn't want to look bad in front of his guests, although it sorrowed him, he had John beheaded and his head placed on a platter and given to Salome, the daughter of Herodias. What we must see in this is the fact that Herod hadn't repented for his sin of being with Herodias, yet he cut off the head of the one calling him to repentance. Herod traded in repentance for a dance! He hadn't turned from his sin, but instead, took a dance in replace of true repentance.

Isn't that the condition of the twenty-first century church? The spirit of Herod is running rampant in God's house. There are so many people replacing repentance with a dance! They're dancing instead of changing, and because of the way they feel while they're doing it, they believe that God approves of it.

Herod lost the head in a dance. There are so many people in the body of Christ that are losing the head (Jesus Christ) dancing! Their dance is detached from the headship of Christ. So many are dancing, but they're not truly repenting, and Jesus refuses to sanction unrepentant praise. Praise is supposed to glorify God, and the only praise that glorifies him is praise given out of a repentant heart.

After the dance, Herod continued in his sin of adultery with Herodias, his brother Phillip's wife. Those that praise God out of the spirit of Herod, after all of their dancing, after all of their shouting, after all of their sweating, crying, and running around the church, will still go home and sleep with their boyfriend or girlfriend. They'll still live compromising lives. They'll still talk to and treat their husband or wife in a demeaning way. Ultimately, after the dance, they'll still leave the house of God and go right back to their sin!

Why is that so? Because in their praise, they lost the head. When you praise God with the head, he'll get in your head. While you're running, he'll tell you to go back and apologize. While you're dancing, he'll tell you to sever that immoral relationship. While you're doing the two-step, he'll tell you to throw away the cigarette pack. When you really praise God with the head, he'll get in your head, while you're praising him.

Herod also, in type, speaks of church leadership. Preachers and pastors: don't lose the head for a dance. Don't always think that you have to preach "feel good" messages that make folks dance and get excited and run around the church. Remember that it's your responsibility to make sure your people are dancing with the head, not just dancing. You're going to have to be willing to preach Jordan messages—messages that cause folks to see themselves, repent and change.

The Head Showed Up and John's Body Matched the Head

The Bible says in the gospel of Matthew that after John had been beheaded, when Herod heard of all the miracles Jesus was working and the word of repentance that he was preaching, Herod thought that Jesus was John the Baptist risen from the dead. (See Matt 14:2.) Jesus and John the Baptist were so closely related in their ministries that Herod believed that Jesus was John.

Why did Herod believe that Jesus was John resurrected? Matthew 14:12 says that John's disciples came and took up his body and buried it; then they went and told Jesus. They buried John's body without a head, because Herodias kept John's head. John's body was buried without the head, and Jesus is the head of the church. The reason why Herod mistook Jesus for John resurrected was because Jesus's head fit John's body! Now I'm speaking to you spiritually and not naturally. The head, Jesus, showed up, and John's body matched it. In other words, John's message of repentance was being preached by Jesus, accompanied with signs, wonders, and miracles. John's body matched Jesus's head.

I suggest to you that John's body, in type, is prophetic for the true body of Christ in the earth. The head, Jesus, is going to show up for the body that looks like John's. Notice that although none of the gospels describe Jesus's earthly body, that they describe John's body. Matthew's gospel says, "And the same John had his raiment of camel's hair, and a leathern girdle about his loins, and his meat was locust and wild honey" (Matt. 3:4).

When the head (Jesus) comes back, he's going to be looking for a body that looks like John's: a body that calls the church to repentance, that preaches a Word of repentance, and that lives a life or perpetual repentance. Jesus said, "Foxes have holes, and birds of the air have nests, but the son of man have no place to lay his head" (Matt. 8:20). There are many bodies (churches) that the head isn't going to lay on! There are many bodies doing many things, helping people have their best life, helping people become a better "you," helping people prosper, but ultimately, the body that will match the head that's coming back for a church without spot or wrinkle or any such thing, will be a church that ministers out of the spirit of repentance. It will be one that continuously calls God's people to renew their minds.

Judas Betrayed Jesus

The role of Judas in the betrayal of Jesus ties directly into everything we've been studying concerning praise and worship. The meaning of Judas is "praised." The name Judas is a derivative, and it is directly connected to the name Judah, which means "praise." Judas's name is directly correlated to praise. As simple as that may seem, it's a groundbreaking revelation. Judas in type is praise personified—the one who betrayed Jesus. His betrayal of the Lamb of God speaks to us of how the Enemy is coming against the church through praise and worship. Judas (praise) is what betrayed Jesus. Praise is what handed Jesus over to the Gentiles. The Enemy uses praise to betray the Savior!

There Are Two Types of Praise: Judah Praise and Judas Praise

Key to our understanding is that there are two types of praise. There is Judah praise, and there is Judas praise. Judas kissed Jesus. Either type of praise can involve kissing the savior. But Judas was kissing Jesus to betray him. In other words, many in the church don't kiss Jesus out of commitment to him, but they kiss (praise) him because they know they're going to betray him when they leave the sanctuary. Many praise him because they know they're still going to live in the sin he died to wash them from. They're still going to live in an attitude Jesus died to change. If we're going to kiss (praise) him and be just as stubborn as we were before we exalted him, we're giving God Judas praise, and not Judah praise! Praise and worship of God without obedience is an act of treason and betrayal.

Judas Praisers Will Always Hand the Lord over to the Gentiles

The book of Acts says of Judas, 'he was guide to them that took Jesus" (Acts 1:16). The Bible says that Judas was guide to them that took Jesus. Don't miss that, because it's imperative to recognize how the Enemy is deceiving us through praise and worship. A guide is a leader, one whom others are led by. "For as many as are led by the Spirit of God, they are the sons of God" (Rom. 8:14).

Judas praise is a false type of the Holy Spirit! Judas praisers actually believe that their praise is the way to Jesus, and not repentance! John (the ministry of repentance) prepares the way for the Lord, not praise. Judas praisers are those who use their praise to get to Jesus although they're living in disobedience to Jesus. Like Herod, they trade in repentance for a dance.

Those who use their dance to replace their obedience unto God always betray Jesus and hand him over to the Gentiles or to those who don't know him. Because of Judas praisers, people who aren't living at all for God think they can come to church and dance and shout, go home and live in sin, selfishness, with no true commitment to serving God, and yet believe they're making their way to Jesus. Entertainers, comedians, secular artists, and athletes that are living in direct opposition to God, believe they can praise and glorify God just like everyone else, because of Judas praisers.

Judas Died Full of Mess after All of That Praise

> For he (Judas) was numbered with us, and had obtained part of this ministry (Acts 1:17).

> Falling head first there, his body split open, spilling out all his intestines (Acts 1:18 NLT).

Judas purchased a field through his betrayal of Jesus, and the Bible declares that he fell headfirst, his body split open, and his bowels spilled out. Bowels are the intestines, the place where we release waste. Our bowel movements come from our bowels. In other words, after all that praise, he ended up dying full of mess. He ended up dying full of sin. He ended up dying full of carnality and worldliness.

CHAPTER 11

TRUE WORSHIP IS FOUND AT THE WELL

Jesus Showed Up at the Well Looking for His Future Bride

He (Jesus) left Judea, and departed again into Galilee. And he must needs go through Samaria. Then cometh he to a city of Samaria, which is called Sy'char ... Now Jacob's well was there. Jesus therefore, being wearied with his journey, sat thus on the well: and it was about the sixth hour. There cometh a woman of Samaria to draw water: Jesus saith unto her, Give me to drink (John 4:3–7).

Wells, which are pits or holes dug into the earth that have a supply of water in them, carry much prophetic meaning all throughout Scripture. One of the main prophetic purposes for wells in the Bible, was that of being a place where a man would meet his future bride. Abraham's servant Eliezar found Isaac's future bride, Rebekah, at a well (Gen. 24:1–27); Jacob found his future bride, Rachel, at a well (Gen. 29:1–14); and Moses found his future bride, Zipporah, at a well (Ex. 2:15–22).

The well speaks of the prophetic place where a man gets a glimpse of the woman who will become his wife. So when Jesus shows up at the well in Samaria, he's not just showing up to get a drink of water—prophetically, he's showing up to meet his future bride. He's showing up at the well to see the bride that is being prepared for him: the church. The woman at the well is a type of the church. Jesus's entire interaction with this woman ties into the well, which, we'll see shortly, has everything to do with worship!

Only Those at the Well Will Be a Part of the Wedding

In this passage from the gospel of John, if you pay close attention to the dialogue between this woman—who is symbolic for the church, the Bride of Christ—and Christ himself, the early narrative focuses on water in the well (John 4:7–14), and the later part shifts to worship in the Spirit (John 4:21–24). Being in the place of the well, the place where you receive refreshing water to quench your thirst and remove the dryness in the mouth and throat, speaks prophetically of being in a place of true worship. True worship is refreshing and will always move you out of the dry places of discouragement, disobedience, disbelief, and anxiety. True worship always removes the dryness. In this passage, Jesus, through his actions, directly connects the well with his future bride. Jesus goes to the well to plan for his wedding.

This revelation is essential. If we're going to be a part of the Bride of Christ, if we're going to see Jesus move in our midst with power and might, and if we're to enter into the kingdom of God, we must understand that only those who stay at the well will be a part of the wedding. Only those who find themselves worshipping Jesus in spirit and truth will make that divine covenant connection with Christ. "God is a Spirit: and they that worship him must worship him in spirit and in truth" (John 4:24). If we're not at the well, we won't be a part of the wedding. If we don't cultivate a place of worship and discipline ourselves to remain in that place, we'll miss his face. To stay at the well, we as believers have to cultivate in our spirits a wail.

The Samaritan Woman Believes That Jesus Needs an Instrument to Draw!

When Jesus asks this Samaritan woman—the church—for a drink of water (in verse 7), prophetically he's asking her for her worship. Jesus above all else desires the worship of his bride. But the problem is that even though she goes to the well often, even though she goes to worship service regularly, even though she is a worshipper, she doesn't know how to worship him. Jesus tells her (in verse 22), "You don't even know what you worship." That's what Jesus is shouting to the church today as well: You don't know what you worship!

Because Babylonian worship has been so influential in the body, in many areas we have begun to lose touch with true worship!

In the gospel of John, the Samaritan woman—prophetically, the church—proves she doesn't understand worship by how she responds when Jesus asks her for a drink of water (worship). "The woman saith unto him, Sir, thou hast nothing to draw with, and the well is deep: from whence then hast thou that living water?" (John 4:11). Thus, she responds by telling Jesus: "You can't get any water (worship), because you have no tool, you have no instrument to draw out water (worship) with." The church's perspective of worship has been so perverted that we believe we can't draw worship out of God's people without an instrument or without music!

The woman at the well says, "Sir, you have nothing to draw water out of the well with, prophetically you have no instrument to draw out worship with, and the well is deep! You have no instrument to cause worship to come forth! You have no means, nothing visible, nothing tangible, to draw out the worship that's buried deep beneath the surface underneath all of people's problems, issues, wants, desires, and distractions!"

The church asks Jesus: How do you expect to get worship without instruments? The church, because of Babylon, believes that worship only goes forth with instruments, praise teams, and choirs. The church believes that Jesus needs an instrument to draw out of his people the worship that he deserves because he died for us.

Jesus Wants to Move Us from Well Worship to Spring Worship

But Jesus, through his interaction with this woman at the well, is attempting to show us a new paradigm of worship and extend our understanding of what true worship really is. He wants to move the boundaries of our worship outside of the walls of music and show us the true divine power and victory that we walk in as we tap into true worship.

"Art thou greater than our father Jacob, which gave us this well, and drank thereof himself, and his children, and his cattle? Jesus answered and said unto her, Whosoever drinketh of this water shall thirst again: But whosoever drinketh of the water that I shall give him shall never thirst; but the water that I shall give him shall be in him a well of water springing up into everlasting life" (John 4:12–14). In this interaction, Jesus says, "Your worship will leave you thirsting again, but the living water, the water I shall give you shall be in you as a well of water, springing up into everlasting life."

In effect, Jesus tells this woman, "Your worship is like a well, while the worship I want to give you is like a spring." In a well, in order to get the water out, or in order to get the worship out, you've got to go down. You've got to dig, and toil with the ground, to get to the water beneath it. He was saying that in order to get your worship out, you've got to use some sort of instrument to penetrate through the fatigue, the stress, the emotions, and attitudes of the people in order to bring worship out of them.

But when you have living water, Jesus says, your worship will be like a spring that springs up. Springs are areas where water comes up out of the earth without any intervention from man! It's water, or worship, that just comes out because there is something going on beneath the surface, because there is something inside the earth that is moving. Living water is when God places a worship on the inside of you that's independent of everything going on around you—it is living water, living worship, worship that remains living when everything around you may be dying.

God desires to give us living water, or living worship. An independent worship! Hallelujah! When somebody is independent, they don't want anyone to help them do anything; they want to do it all on their own. Jesus promises to give us a worship, an adoration, an exaltation of him that doesn't depend on anything else to flow out of our innermost being. It's a worship that works—even when things aren't working for us. It's being able to truly walk in the joy of the Lord.

"Whosoever drinketh of this water shall thirst again" (John 4:13). Worship that is dependent on an instrument to draw it forth will leave you thirsty again. You'll have to come back to the same well to get refreshed. You'll have to go to another concert, revival, conference, or special program just to experience a certain level of worship. But Jesus said, "Believe me, dear woman, the time is coming when it will no longer matter whether you worship the Father on this mountain or in Jerusalem" (John 4:21 NLT). God was saying this: You will be able to experience the same measures of my glory in your personal worship, and in your local church worship, that you experience at your national conferences and meetings. A measure of the same glory you experience at your revivals you'll be able to experience in your bathroom, or the break room on your job, or while you're riding in the car, because your worship won't need an instrument, or a particular place, to flow out of you.

It's worship that doesn't need to go back to the well to be activated.

Has the Church's Worship Become Sterile?

> The woman saith unto him, Sir give me this water, that I thirst not, neither come hither to draw. Jesus saith unto her, Go, call thy husband, and come hither. The woman answered and said, I have no husband. Jesus saith unto her. Thou hast well said, I have no husband: For thou hast had five husbands; and he whom thou now hast is not thy husband (John 4:15–18).

Jesus is yet trying to get this woman to understand that worship isn't just something that we experience or that touches us, but instead it is supposed to produce something in us. By bringing up her many husbands, he says, "You have had five husbands, and the one you're with now isn't your husband." The reason Jesus brought up her husband at the well was because the well is the place where the groom meets his future bride.

She had met husbands in worship, but because she didn't truly understand worship, she'd had five husbands, but no children. Her worship was sterile and lacked the ability to give birth and conceive the things of God. Her worship was impotent; it was barren; it was infertile. God is saying prophetically that much of our worship is barren, lacking the ability to conceive in us greater anointing, greater revelation, greater influence, and greater obedience and submission to God, because we don't know who our husband is.

Jesus told the Samaritan woman, and is saying prophetically to the church: The man that's at your house now isn't your husband. Whatever it is that's touching you when you come together for worship, but is not producing holiness and obedience in you is not your husband! He is not the bridegroom. In this encounter, Jesus knows that whatever man she has at home isn't her husband, because he is. We receive a lot of things packaged in Jesus's name that aren't Jesus. We go to the well and wind up worshipping with a man that's not our husband; as a result, we come out of our worship experience unchanged—and barren.

Water Pots Will Be Dropped in a True Worship Experience

> The woman saith unto him, Sir, I perceive that thou art a prophet … The woman saith unto him, I know that Messiah cometh, which is called Christ: when he is come, he will tell us all things. Jesus saith unto her, I that speak unto thee am he … The woman then left her waterpot, and went her way into the city, and saith to the men. Come, see a man, which told me all things that ever I did: is not this the Christ? Then they went out of the city, and came unto him (Jesus) (John 4:19, 25–30).

Don't forget that Jesus is trying to give us a revelation of worship. The woman— the church—says, I perceive you to be a prophet, in other words, I acknowledge the prophetic office that you operate in and the prophetic gift on your life. Then she says, "When the Messiah comes he will tell us all things." His response to her is "I am he—I'm your future husband." At this, the woman drops her water pot and goes out and tells the men of the city about Jesus.

She came into worship carrying a pot, she left carrying the message of Jesus Christ. That's what happens after true worship goes forth; you'll always drop something you brought in—to free your hands to carry out the commission of Christ for your life. Worship causes you to drop water pots for the sake of carrying the message of the cross. You'll drop your goals. You'll drop your dreams. You'll drop your agendas. You'll drop jobs. You'll drop sin and disobedience. You'll drop everything that hinders you from carrying out the kingdom assignment that God has revealed to you through worship!

That's why I know that when people can't drop problematic habits, patterns, and tendencies after worship, they didn't truly experience worship in the third heaven where God dwells (see chapter 6). Instead, their worship was in the first heaven where spiritual wickedness resides. True worship will provoke you to drop your water pots without anybody telling you to. Jesus didn't tell her to drop the water pot; when she saw him for who he was, when she saw the Messiah, she dropped it on her own! It's impossible to see him without forgetting about you! When you enter into true worship, you don't enter in and gain for yourself, you enter in and lose more of yourself. You leave declaring, "I am crucified with Christ: It is no longer I who live, but Christ lives in me" (Gal. 2:20).

True Worship Overflows into Witnessing

In her worship, she saw Christ. And right after seeing him, she went out and drew people unto him. Her worship made her a witness! Remember, worship is about drawing people unto him. She says to the men of the city, after experiencing true worship, "Come see a man that told me everything I ever did!" (John 4:29). And then "they went out of the city, and came unto him" (John 4:30).

God wants us to understand that when we tap into true worship, it will provoke us into being a witness! We won't simply want to come out of worship talking about the good time that we had and be looking forward to doing it again, but we'll leave the worship experience with a grace on us to witness to others the truth we ourselves just witnessed. Satan's Babylonian system of worship, which emphasizes music, wants the church to isolate worship within the confines of the music and a worship service so we never gain the understanding that our worship is supposed to overflow into our witness.

True Worship Satisfies Jesus

> In the mean while his disciples prayed him, saying, Master, eat. But he said unto them, I have meat to eat that ye know not of. Therefore said the disciples one to another, Hath any man brought him ought to eat? Jesus saith unto them, My meat is to do the will of him that sent me, and to finish his work (John 4:31–34).

After the woman dropped her pot and went out and told the men of the city about Jesus, the disciples came and offered him food and more than likely water to go with it, and Jesus refused it. That should stand out to you, because earlier we had been told that Jesus had been famished from his journey—hungry and thirsty. But, after interacting with the Samaritan woman, he says, "I have meat that you know not of." He didn't want any food or water, although no one had given him any. Why? Because true worship refreshes the Lord! He had gotten what he was thirsty for: genuine worship. Worship in which water pots are dropped!

At the beginning of their dialogue, the woman told Jesus, "You have no instrument to draw with" (verse 11). What she didn't realize is that *she* was the instrument. God wants us to understand that we don't need instruments to worship, but we become instruments when we worship! Worship makes us witnesses. Worship makes us instruments by which Jesus draws people unto himself! Jesus said, *If I be lifted up, I'll draw all men unto myself* (John 12:32). After the woman's witness, all of the men of the city came unto Jesus. Her worship made her a witness; it made her the instrument that drew people unto Christ!

After his interaction with the woman at the well, Jesus immediately began talking about the harvest: "You know the saying, 'Four months between planting and harvest.' But I say, wake up and look around. The fields are already ripe for harvest. The harvesters are paid good wages, and the fruit they harvest is people brought unto eternal life" (John 4:35–36 NLT). Worship has a direct influence on bringing in the harvest. If our worship isn't pure, the harvest will be prolonged. There are souls that won't be brought unto eternal life until we, the body of Christ do the work of washing our worship, and coming out of Babylon. The Enemy works diligently to always be included in our worship, because he is trying to hold back the harvest.

As we'll see in our next chapter, the Enemy always desires to put his hand in our worship so as to pervert and pollute the harvest of the Lord.

CHAPTER 12

THE CHURCH CAN'T USE FLESH HOOKS!

Now the sons of Eli were corrupt, they did not know the Lord. And the priests' custom with the people was that when any man offered a sacrifice, the priest's servant would come with a three-pronged fleshhook in his hand while the meat was boiling. Then he would thrust it into the pan, or kettle, or caldron, or pot, and the priest would take for himself all that the fleshhook brought up (1 Sam. 2:12–17 NKJV).

So the Philistines fought and Israel was defeated, and every man fled to his tent. There was a very great slaughter, and there fell of Israel thirty thousand foot soldiers. Also the Ark of God was captured; and the two sons of Eli, Hophni and Phinehas, died (1 Sam. 4:10–11 NKJV).

God's Presence and Sacrifice

One thing that should stand out to us as we read the Book of First Samuel is that chapter 2 deals with the sacrifice of the Lord being perverted by the priests, while chapter 4 deals with the loss of the ark, the place where God's Manifest Presence resided. When I refer to God's Manifest Presence, I'm referring to his visible presence that can be recognized by our senses. We can feel him, see him, and know that he is among us. I don't mean his omnipresence, which is in all places at all times, whether people are aware that he is there or not. The ark of God represented God's Manifest Presence, for he would come down and sit on the mercy seat on the Day of Atonement, and all of Israel knew he was there through the visible clouds, smoke, and fire. Thus, directly after the loss of pure sacrifice came the loss of God's tangible presence (the ark of God). That indicates to us that maintaining proper sacrifice unto God is inextricably tied to maintaining God's Manifest Presence. Without proper sacrifice, the presence of God will lift—which means that the Manifest Presence is released through sacrifice.

Various parts of the Bible inform us about the Manifest Presence. On Mount Carmel, God's Presence came down in the form of a fire and consumed Elijah's sacrifice after he placed it on the altar (see 1 Kings 18:30–40). When Solomon had built the temple, he gave multiple sacrifices to dedicate the temple, and according to Second Chronicles, "When Solomon had made an end of praying, the fire came down from heaven, and consumed the burnt offering and the sacrifices: and the glory of the Lord filled the house. And the priests could not enter into the house of the Lord, because the glory of the Lord [the Manifest Presence] had filled the house" (2 Chron. 7:1–3). Also, we learn that on the Day of Atonement, the high priest would only enter into the Most Holy Place, where God's Presence sat on the ark of the covenant, after sacrificing a bullock for his sins and another animal for the sins of the people (Lev. 16:1-34; Heb. 7:27).

The requirement of sacrifice wasn't altered by Jesus's death on the cross. Under the New Testament we're yet required to give God proper sacrifice if we're going to experience His Presence. Although the requirement of sacrifice hasn't changed from the Old Testament to the New Testament, what God has required for us to sacrifice has. During the times of the patriarchs, they were required to sacrifice animals for God's Presence; we who are New Testament believers are required to sacrifice ourselves.

"Present your bodies a living sacrifice, holy, acceptable unto God" (Rom. 12:1). We're called to experience God's Presence as we sacrifice ourselves. We must understand that the animal sacrificial system of the Old Testament is a type and shadow of the New Testament calling of the sacrifice of self. So the animal sacrifice of the Old Covenant always speaks prophetically of the sacrifice of self.

The offering of the animal sacrifice unto God is a type of us offering ourselves unto God. The second chapter of First Samuel speaks prophetically to us about the many people in the church who have offered themselves unto God improperly, which has led to the absence of God's Presence in the church.

God's Presence Is Hindered by Priests Who Use Flesh Hooks

> Now the sons of Eli were sons of Belial; they knew not the Lord … when any man offered sacrifice, the priest's servant came, while the flesh was in seething [boiling], with a fleshhook of three teeth in his hand (1 Sam. 2:12–14).

The Bible shows that when men gave their sacrifice—prophetically this refers to men and woman of God, laying down their lives in sacrificial service unto Jesus—the priest would send his servant in with a three-pronged flesh hook to take the sacrifice out of the pot before it was done being cooked. The Bible says they did this because *these priests didn't know the Lord!* (See 1 Sam. 2:12.) We must understand that everybody teaching Christ doesn't necessarily know Christ! More specifically, Eli's sons didn't know the ways of the Lord. There are so many in the church who attempt to teach the way *to* the Lord but don't know the ways *of* the Lord.

The proof that they didn't know the ways of the Lord was that they were taking the sacrifices out of the boiling pot before they were fully prepared. The priests, the leaders of the church, the covering of God's people, were only supposed to pull the sacrifice out of the pot after it seethed or boiled in the pot long enough to be done. That's the challenge we are having in the body of Christ.

Putting the sacrifice in the pot was a part of God's plan and process for preparing it! The church has many living sacrifices, many people who come to the church who are going through fiery trials and furnace-like circumstances. They have been placed in the pot by God, so they can get done! So they can be done with sin. Done with compromise. Done with self and pride. Done with unbelief. Done with disobedience. Done with carnality and worldliness.

The pot was necessary for *purpose* to be fulfilled. We can't begin purpose until we're done with ourselves! Living sacrifices that don't stay in the pot will never fulfill their purpose, because they'll never be totally done with themselves. The pot speaks of the necessary suffering God allows us to go through to sanctify and purify our motives and to bring us to the place in which we're done with us so that we can follow him: Jesus.

> So then, since Christ suffered physical pain, you must arm yourselves with the same attitude he had, and be ready to suffer, too. For if you have suffered physically for Christ, you have finished with sin. You won't spend the rest of your lives chasing your own desires, but you will be anxious to do the will of God (1 Peter 4:1–2 NLT).

In the New English Translation, the verse about one's own desires says, "In that he spends the rest of his time on earth concerned about the will of God and not human desires" (1 Peter 4:2 NET).

We can never be given over totally to the will of God until we suffer in every area we're living for the will of man! Every sacrifice must be put in the pot. Every sacrifice must go through seething. The pot is necessary to bring us from the place of simply focusing on Jesus's sacrifice for us to becoming a living sacrifice for him! "In this you greatly rejoice, though now for a little while you may have had to suffer grief in all kinds of trials. These have come so that your faith-of greater worth than gold, which perishes even though refined by fire-may be proved genuine" (1 Peter 1:6–7 NIV).

Sometimes When We Pull People Out of Their Problems, We're Actually Pulling Them Out of Their Process

Now, understanding the necessity of the pot to bring the sacrifice to the point where it is done—prophetically, the pot symbolizing our suffering, and the sacrifice typifying us who are called to be living sacrifices—we can see the detriment behind what Eli's sons, Hophni and Phinehas, were doing.

The Bible's account of the sin of Eli's sons was presented earlier. Here is another translation of that passage:

> Whenever anyone offered a sacrifice, Eli's sons would send over a servant with a three-pronged fork (flesh hook). While the meat of the sacrificed animal was still boiling the servant would stick the fork into the pot and demand that whatever it brought up be given to Eli's sons (1 Sam. 2:13–14 NLT).

Because they didn't know the way of the Lord (see verse 12), they were using their position to pull the sacrifices out of the pot although God had ordained that they stay in until they were done. This speaks prophetically of all of the many priests or preachers in the body of Christ who are using their position to try to preach God's people out of pots that God himself has ordained for them to be in!

God uses the pot to prepare us for purpose, but when we don't know the way of the Lord, which is suffering, we'll try to pull people out of their pot before God is done with them. We wind up pulling them out of their process! We try to preach to people that things are going to get better, instead of preaching to them that God has them there to make their attitude better even while things get worse. We'll preach to people that they're coming out of the pot of unrighteous and unfair bosses and managers, instead of preaching that God has them there to learn how to honor authority that they don't agree with. We'll preach to people that God is going to smite their enemies, instead of preaching to them: The reason enemies are all around you is because God is trying to teach you how to love them.

Because we're in the midst of a Hophni and Phinehas generation of leadership that doesn't understand the way of the Lord, we're pulling people out of the pot before God is done with them. So people come out of their pot without coming out of themselves. They come out of their suffering without sanctification. They're told that they can leave where they are without being told that it means they'll stay in their flesh. Remember, Babylon is a worship system that desires to bring you into an encounter with heaven without requiring you to come out of your flesh (see chapter 6).

Many true prophets, teachers, and seers have gotten so drunk through Babylon that they've become prophets of Baal. They are prophets who constantly give a word that promises a change but doesn't require any! They are false teachers and false prophets who always preach of how God wants to change what's *around* you instead of how God is using what's around you to change something *in* you.

The treasure is in earthen vessels (see 2 Cor. 4:7). The pot, the fiery trial that's around us, is to dig out all the dirt that's keeping people from seeing the treasure that the Lord has invested in us. "For I reckon that the sufferings of this present time are not worthy to be compared with the glory which shall be revealed in us" (Rom. 8:18). Zion, we must wake back up to the way of the Lord. The way of the Lord is repentance and humility.

Flesh Hooks

These priests were using a flesh hook to bring sacrifices unto themselves. This speaks prophetically of what's taking place in the body of Christ right now. It speaks of preachers who are hooking people—bringing in massive crowds, and establishing large ministries—through the use of flesh hooks. These ministries are receiving unprepared sacrifices. They are willing to receive your life without requiring you to lay your life down. Many in the church world today are hooking folks into the church who aren't truly hooked on Christ.

Instead of hooking you on laying down your life because Jesus laid down his life for you, you're hooked by a church giving you something that you like in your unregenerate current condition. The church hooks you by using music you like to already listen to. Or it hooks you by acting the way you act or dressing the way you dress. It hooks you by focusing on individuality more than conformity. All of these are flesh hooks.

It's a trick of the Enemy. If I've got to give you something you like in your flesh for you to come to Christ, then in reality you never came to Christ. "If any man would come after, let him deny himself, take up his cross, and follow me" (Matt. 16:24). The first thing we must do in order to follow Christ is to deny ourselves, which means that if I hook you with self, you may come to church, but you will never come to Christ!

The problem we're having is that the Enemy has used Babylon to get us so drunk that he has deceived us into believing that we can use self—use flesh—to draw people to Christ. He has gotten us to use flesh hooks. The problem with flesh hooks is that they'll hook you when you are only half done. Hophni and Phinehas pulled out the sacrifice from the boiling pot before it was completely done. The Enemy is getting the church to hook people who aren't holy. These are people who are not hooked on sacrificial living. The Babylonian spirit has the church hooking people by giving them something that they already had, so in actuality, they simply got hooked on themselves and not on Christ.

The Enemy knows that if you get hooked by flesh, you'll remain hooked on flesh! That's why there are so many people who are hooked on church—are faithful in attendance—but yet are hooked on sin. Jesus says in the gospel of John, "That which is born of flesh can only produce flesh, and that which is born of the Spirit can only produce Spirit" (John 3:6). It's impossible for me to hook you in your flesh and expect you to walk after the spirit.

"For all who are led by the Spirit of God are the children of God" (Rom. 8:14). This means that there are masses of people who are a part of the church but who are not God's children. I say this truth with trembling and grief. If the Enemy continues to deceive the church into using flesh hooks, he'll succeed in getting us hooked on something carnal so we can't walk in anything spiritual.

The Flesh Hook Will Always Have Three Prongs

Whenever anyone offered a sacrifice, Eli's sons would send over a servant with a three-pronged fork. While the meat of the sacrificed animal was still boiling, the servant would stick the fork into the pot (1 Sam. 2:13–14 NLT).

The priest would use a fork of three prongs to bring the sacrifice out of the boiling pot before it was done. This is speaking prophetically of the false ministry of Babylon. We can't forget that Babylon poses as the Bride of Christ; she is the false bride, pretending to do the work of the true bride.

The fork had three prongs because it speaks prophetically of the false trinity! It's the Enemy coming as an angel of light, acting as if he's doing the work of the Father, the Son, and the Holy Spirit, when in actuality he's doing the work of Satan, the beast, and the false prophet! (See Rev. 16:13.)

The Babylon Bride seems as if she's pulling you out of your problems, but she's actually pulling you out of your purpose! The false bride works diligently to pull God's people out of God ordained fires that are necessary to fulfill God's purpose. These trials are absolutely irreplaceable in aligning us with the will of God for our lives. God's will and God's kingdom are inextricably tied together. If we're pulled out of these pots, we'll be pulled out of the kingdom! "Not everyone who calls out to me, 'Lord! Lord!' will enter the Kingdom of Heaven. Only those who actually do the will of my Father in heaven will enter" (Matt. 7:21 NLT).

The Devil has taken advantage of many in the church today because we no longer understand the value of suffering, dying to self, and being refined, so when the Devil puts a flesh hook down in our pot, down in our struggle, and tells us we don't deserve to go through what we're going through, or we're not supposed to be dealing with what we're dealing with, then like a fish we take the bait and get pulled out of our God-ordained pot prematurely. This happens without us ever understanding or allowing God to do the necessary work he desires to do in us while we're in it. We see it all as the Enemy's work and never as God working on us. So the Enemy gets us to trade in eternal purpose for temporary relief. He gets us to abort our refining process by getting us to believe that we're coming out of something he put us in—while in reality we're coming out of something that God placed us in.

So instead of following God, we'll actually wind up following Satan. To follow is to worship. This means that many will be worshipping Satan, all the time believing that they are worshipping Jehovah God! Babylon uses flesh hooks to keep us in this world. The Bible declares in Revelation, "And all the people who belong to this world worshiped the beast. They are the ones whose names were not written in the Book of Life before the world was made" (Rev. 13:8).

Flesh hooks get us to write on the church roll the names of individuals whose names aren't written in the Book of Life! Jesus said that this deceptive false ministry would be so convincing *that even the very chosen of God would barely escape its alluring and deceptive weapons* (see Matt. 24).

All Sacrifices Must Have the Fat Consumed

> Sometimes the servant would come even before the animal's fat had been burned on the altar. He would demand raw meat before it had been boiled so that it could be used for roasting. The man offering the sacrifice might reply, "Take as much as you want, but the fat must be burned first." Then the servant would demand, "No, give it to me now, or I'll take it by force" (1 Sam. 2:15–16 NLT).

Not only did Hophni and Phinehas pervert the sacrifice by receiving it unprepared, but they also required those who were offering their sacrifices to leave the fat. This was in direct rebellion to the Levitical law as to how the priests were to receive sacrifice. They were never to receive sacrifice with fat on it.

> If his offering is a goat he must present it before the Lord, lay his hand on its head, and slaughter it before the Meeting Tent, and the sons of Aaron must splash its blood against the altar's sides. Then he must present from it his offering as a gift to the Lord: the fat which covers the entrails and all the fat on the entrails ... Then the priest must offer them up in smoke on the altar as a food gift for a soothing aroma-all the fat belongs to the Lord. This is a perpetual statute throughout your generations in all the places where you live: You must never eat any fat or any blood (Lev. 3:12–17 NET).

God commanded the priests to never receive any sacrifice in which the entirety of the fat had not been removed. Prophetically, they were never to receive someone as a living sacrifice—someone as a true, born-again believer—if they hadn't removed all of their fat. All the fat was to be burned on the altar unto the Lord. God said to burn it on the altar, because the fat belongs to him.

Fat in Scripture speaks of excess, or having more than what is necessary. When an individual is in a state of obesity, it means that they have on them more weight than what they need to live. Part of presenting ourselves as a sacrifice unto the Lord is being willing to lay our fat on the altar. God requires our fat. He wants us to give him those things that we have above our necessity. God wants our excess time, money, abilities, and gifts for his purposes. God wants our overflow. He requires our fat—not to the point where we don't enjoy our blessings, but to the point where we commit our blessings unto him.

The current-day "priests" (pastors and preachers) are receiving sacrifices who aren't willing to give the overflow of their lives unto God. These "sacrifices" are people who believe that they have done their duty to God and the church by coming to Sunday morning service, leaving, and then going on with their lives. It speaks of the popular mentality of the modern church that never considers sacrificing one's weekends, free-time, hobbies, personal agendas, and the like to help further the vision of the house of which they are a part.

They believe that church is about encouraging them in their personal pursuits and isn't to interfere with their fat but is to help them gain more fat. They don't look at the church as the place where we as believers are called to lay down our life.

The problem is that Babylonian leaders are accepting this outlook. As a result, people come to Christ, and join the church, believing that their fat doesn't belong to God, but to them. These people will actually be offended when the church wants their fat—their time, talent, money, and personal agendas—and admonishes them to lay down their lives.

In the Old Testament times, if the priest accepted a sacrifice with the fat, God wouldn't accept that sacrifice. Today, there are multitudes of people being received by pastors but whom God refuses to receive because they are being received even though they're not willing to let go of their fat for Christ.

The reason why these two wicked priests, Hophni and Phinehas, were willing to pervert the sacrifices by receiving undone sacrifices with the fat was because they were to receive a certain portion of every animal sacrifice given. For every sacrifice brought in, they got something out of it. In twenty-first century terms: For every member that joins, for every new tither, for every new body on the pew, the pastor gets something out of it. Pastors under the influence of the Babylonian spirit don't mind receiving undone, unprepared sacrifices—in other words, receiving folks who are unprepared to live lives of sacrifice—because they know that they'll get something out of it.

The Sacrifice Was to Be Eaten in the Holy Place

How does this pervert the sacrifice? "Every male among the priests shall eat thereof: it shall be eaten in the holy place: it is most holy" (Lev. 7:6). For every sacrifice that was brought to the priests to be offered unto the Lord, there were certain portions of that sacrifice—outside of the two kidneys, the fat, and the caul above the liver—that the priests had the God-given right to eat. We can't overlook this, because there is prophetic weight attached.

God ordained that the priest could eat a portion of the sacrifice, with one condition: that it be eaten in the holy place. The priest eating the sacrifice brought by the people is prophetic for the priest receiving that sacrifice into his body. His eating the sacrifice prophetically signified that that sacrifice was being received into the body. It was a foreshadowing of our high priest receiving us into his body. The priest's receiving the sacrifice into the body came with one requirement, that it be received only in the holy place. He was forbidden to receive that sacrifice into the body until that sacrifice was brought into a holy place.

Our challenge in the church is not our accepting of new souls into the body. The church has more members in the body now than ever in history. The problem is where we are accepting them. Many of these new members, these living sacrifices, have been accepted in the wrong place. They aren't living in holiness; they aren't walking in righteousness; they haven't even turned their back on their sin and iniquity. There are too many people coming to the church—to Christ—as a sacrifice, and we're receiving them into the body, we're receiving their offering, outside of the holy place! Being holy is being set apart for, and living your life exclusively for, God alone. We're receiving individuals into the body that haven't even made up their mind to live exclusively for God.

The Churches' Life of sacrifice Has Caused People To Despise, Being a Living Sacrifice

"Wherefore the sin of the young men was very great before the Lord: for men abhorred the offering of the Lord" (1 Sam. 2:17). Because of the perversion of the sacrifice of Eli's two sons, the Bible declares, men abhorred the sacrifice. To abhor something is to despise, detest, hate, revile, or undervalue it. Also, to disregard, neglect, or see no use in. Because of these two priests, God's people saw no use in sacrificing unto the Lord.

Because men were allowed to offer unsanctified sacrifice, the sacrifice of the Lord was despised by men. What does that say to us prophetically today? Because so many people are being received into the body who aren't truly done with themselves, people see no true value in being living sacrifices with a focus on laying ourselves down for the sake of the kingdom.

That's the condition of the church today. There are droves of people in the Christian community who undervalue and disregard sacrificial living, and it's all because the church has received so many unprepared sacrifices that are living their lives outside of the holy place! Because people are allowed to offer unsanctified sacrifice to the church today, the sacrifice of the Lord is despised by men! People don't want to completely offer their lives unto the Lord, or don't see any use in it, because we have so many half-done sacrifices in the church. People see no point or value in truly laying down all of their sin and carnality before entering into the body of Christ. In many cases, the church's lack of sacrifice has caused people to despise being living sacrifices.

No Sanctification, No Open Revelation

There is a direct correlation that the loss of pure sacrifice has with the loss of God's Presence. Immediately following the description of the apostasy in sacrifice, First Samuel says, "And the child Samuel ministered unto the Lord before Eli. And the word of the Lord was precious in those days; there was no open vision" (1 Sam. 3:1). The New Living Translation says, "Now in those days messages from the Lord were very rare, and visions were quite uncommon." The New Century Version says, "In those days the Lord did not speak directly to people very often there were very few visions."

Notice that when describing the spiritual condition of Israel, the Scripture begins by saying, "In those days." This means that in the days of unsanctified sacrifice, God rarely spoke directly to his people and rarely gave any revelation of himself! Because of all the unsanctified sacrifice, there were very few encounters with God's Manifest Presence.

God Wants Us to Walk with His Presence, Not to Have to Go and Fetch It

Chapter 4 of the first book of Samuel shows us the ultimate result of unsanctified sacrifice and how it connects with the loss of God's Presence. In that book, the Bible tells of how Israel went into battle against the Philistines and lost four thousand men in battle. What we can't overlook is their response after being defeated by their enemy.

The people of Israel came to the conclusion that they lost the battle because they had gone into it without the ark of God. They said, "Let us go fetch the arc of God and then we can defeat our enemy" (1 Sam. 4:3). This shows the problem with unsanctified sacrifice—those individuals who aren't living a life set apart for the Lord. They want to carry the ark of God, God's Presence, into their battles, but have no desire to carry his Presence daily. They don't want to live the necessary life of daily sacrifice so that they can carry his Presence on a daily basis.

Israel had to go fetch the ark—go and get the Presence of God—instead of already having it with them. Too many times we wait until a catastrophe or devastation rocks the stability of our lives before we fervently seek the face of the Lord through prayer, his Word, and church attendance. We find ourselves having to go fetch the ark in order to face an enemy. God, however, desires for us to walk with him. He wants to be with us when we enter into a trial, so we'll have the faith to know that he'll be with us until we come out of it. We don't want to have to go and try to fetch the ark and fight at the same time.

When we're babes, God will allow us to operate on this level, but eventually he'll require us to become sons, and sons walk with the Father. If we continue to try to take his Presence into battle without taking up our cross daily, we'll eventually find ourselves in a battle in which he makes none of his divine virtue available for us to fight with! This is what happened to Israel.

It is significant that although Israel was operating under leadership that didn't know God's way and was accepting unsanctified sacrifice, Israel was yet able to fetch the ark of God. Through prophetic hindsight, we can see that they were able to bring a form of godliness into their midst (2 Tim. 3:5). They had the ark, which was the form of God's presence, but they didn't have the power of his Manifest Presence to give them victory over their enemy. There was a sense that God was present with them, through a form, but as we'll see in a moment, indeed his Manifest Presence was not. There are churches in which there are forms of God's Presence experienced through the music, through the singing, and through the presentations of God given in church. It may be a congregation in which many haven't truly given their lives over to the Lord or his work! God will show up in their form, even in places where the leadership doesn't know who he is, because he loves his church that much, and his mercy endures forever.

The first book of Samuel states that when the ark, when God's Presence, entered into the midst of the people, a *shabach* praise broke out. God's people went up into a high praise. They began to shout, dance, and glorify God with such intensity that their praise literally shook the ground and could be heard in the camp of Israel's enemy (see 1 Sam. 4:5–8).

It sounds like they were having some good church. They were having a Pentecostal revival. But after all that praising and shouting, and even though they had the ark with them, they still lost the battle! Why? Their shout was unsanctified! An unsanctified shout might encourage us, but it can't defeat an enemy. The power of shouting and praising God is released only through sanctified lips—lips of individuals who have laid down their lives for the kingdom. That's the shout that can heal bodies, cast out demons, turn around families, and deliver our children. The shouts of the unsanctified get us excited but have no power to defeat any enemy!

Israel was defeated, and the enemy took the ark from them. Israel lost God's Presence directly after giving him high praise. Praise doesn't make a difference without holiness.

In the next chapter, we'll examine some more of the characteristics of true and false worship by reviewing what the Philistines did when they took the ark, in which dwelled the very Presence of God.

Chapter 13

We Can't Have God's Presence and Hemorrhoids

Based on the chapter title, I know you may be saying, "This preacher has to be crazy, what in the world does God's Presence have to do with hemorrhoids?" Don't close this book just yet. The Bible itself is what brings up the subject of hemorrhoids. I promise that if you just hear me out, you'll be better able to discern between true worship and Babylonian worship—and between the true Presence of God and the artificial presence that Babylonian worship attempts to produce!

Sin and the Savior

> And the ark of God was taken; and the two sons of Eli, Hoph'ni and Phin'e-has were slain. And the Philistines took the ark of God, and brought it from Ebenezer unto Ashdod. When the Philistines took the ark of God, they brought it into the house of Dagon, and set it by Dagon (1 Sam. 4:11; 5:1–2).

It's interesting to note the fact that after the Philistines defeated Israel, they took the ark. We can't overlook that, because we understand that the ark was affiliated with the Presence of God. The Philistines, who were the enemy of God's people, wanted God's Presence.

The Philistines were uncircumcised, in other words they were deemed unfit to worship God, yet they sought out the Presence of God. The Philistines typologically represent a large portion of the church that desire God's Presence even though they're not in covenant relationship with him. These people are living in sin, compromise, and worldliness yet want to benefit from and experience God's Presence. They want to live an ungodly life yet claim access to God's Presence.

Dagon Worship Has No Right to God's Presence

The way in which the Philistines set the ark, God's Presence, in the temple of Dagon helps us understand how those who are not in covenant with God attempt to worship God. The Bible indicates that the Philistines set the ark, God's Presence, next to their false idol god Dagon. Their actions suggest that they thought man-made worship had a place in God's Presence.

Their placing a man-made form of worship near the Presence of God speaks to us prophetically of the idea that man-made worship has a place in ushering in the Presence of God. Today, there is still Dagon worship. This occurs when lukewarm, self-motivated musicians, who haven't died to themselves, believe that they can create a glory, or release God's Presence, through how they play with their hands, even though those hands are unclean. Or it occurs when worship is focused more on an experience than on edification.

False worship is when we place more emphasis on practice and preparation than we do on cultivating a pure and obedient heart unto God. We focus on how musicians play more than how they pray. We focus more on their singing than on their sanctification. We focus more on how people respond when the music is playing than how Christlike their lives are when the music stops.

We, the church, have been very much guilty of this very thing. The Bible story of Dagon speaks prophetically of the manufactured worship that is so prevalent and popular in the body, worship that many individuals actually believe can gain true access to God's Divine Presence. Just like the Philistines, many of us set up Dagon, man-made worship, next to the ark, God's Presence.

The Philistines left Dagon before the ark of God overnight, and when they came into the temple of Dagon the next morning, something profound had taken place, something that speaks to us about God's perspective on man-made worship.

> But when the citizens of Ashdod went to see it the next morning, Dagon had fallen with his face to the ground in front of the Ark of the Lord! So they took Dagon and put him in his place again. But the next morning the same thing happened—Dagon had fallen, face down before the Ark of the Lord again. This time his head and hands had broken off and were lying in the doorway. Only the trunk of his body was left intact (1 Sam. 5:3 NLT).

I have heard interpretations of this text from the perspective that the reason Dagon had fallen face down before the ark was because God was declaring that he is the only true and living God, which I totally agree with. But if we look at this text from a prophetic perspective, it tells us that many individuals believe that man-made worship has a place before the Presence of Almighty God. Dagon fell face down before the ark of God. He was in a posture of worship. Dagon falling before the ark speaks prophetically of the gross misunderstanding that says we can have access to God's Presence within ourselves no matter what standard of life we're living.

The second night Dagon is set before the Lord, God gives us a revelation as to his response to man's belief that man-made worship has any place in his presence. In the morning, the citizens found that the idol "had fallen, face down before the Ark of the Lord again" and that "his head and hands had broken off and were lying in the doorway" (1 Sam. 5:3 NLT). God's response to the belief that man-made worship could enter into his presence was having Dagon's head and hands cut off at the doorway. In worship, our hands are what we're called to lift up as a symbol of our surrender to God. Dagon's hands were cut off at the entrance of the doorway. Although Dagon's stump had entered into the temple or church, his hands, his worship, was left at the doorway!

God is saying prophetically that there are many who are coming into the house of God whose worship isn't being accepted by him. There are people whom God is telling, "You have to check your worship at the door, because it's unclean!" God wants us to understand that all worship doesn't qualify to enter into his Presence.

We can come into the house of God without entering into God's Presence. Man-manipulated worship can never manipulate God! "Be not deceived, God is not mocked" (Gal. 6:7). When Dagon fell, the impact of the fall caused his hands to be cut off. You can always tell those who are worshippers under a Dagon anointing, because when things in life fall, they can't keep their arms up. Those who aren't true worshipers don't know how to maintain their worship in the wilderness.

Many Churchgoers Are Men at the Top but Still Fish at the Bottom

"Only the stump of Dagon was left to him" (1 Sam. 5:4). The Bible says that when man-made worship attempted to enter into the Presence of the Lord, Dagon's hands and head were cut off, and the only thing left before God's Presence was Dagon's stump. To understand what God is attempting to communicate to us through this, we must understand that Dagon was an idol god whose upper half was in the shape of a man, while his lower half was in the form of a fish. Dagon's anatomy helps us to understand how God sees carnal worshippers. Dagon's form represents individuals who are worshippers at the top, or on the surface, but they're still fish at the bottom, or underneath the surface!

Jesus told Peter and Andrew, "Follow me, and I'll make you to become fishers of men" (Matt. 4:19). Jesus refers to men who are yet to come unto salvation, or who are yet to receive their redemption, as fish. Why? Because they still need to be caught by God. They still need to be hooked on God.

When we're operating under Dagonic (which is demonic) worship, although we may be worshipping God on the surface, at church, we still haven't been captured by God beneath the surface, or in the areas of our lives that no one else can see. These are people who aren't hooked on personal prayer, hooked on personal consecration, hooked on personal study of the Word, or hooked on being led by the Spirit.

They don't spend their personal time seeking out God's daily will for their lives but instead seek their own will. They don't truly give God much of their private life but believe their public worship makes up for that! These lukewarm believers are worshippers at the top. But God sees they are still fish at the bottom!

Emerods Are Hemorrhoids

> But the hand of the Lord was heavy upon them of Ashdod, and he destroyed them, and smote them with emerods ... And when the men of Ashdod saw that it was so, they said, The ark of the God of Israel shall not abide with us: for his hand is sore upon us, and upon Dagon our god ... And it was so, that after they had carried it about, the hand of the Lord was against the city with a great destruction: and he smote the men of the city, both small and great, and they had emerods in their secret parts (1 Sam. 5:6–9).

The word *emerods* we today know as *hemorrhoids*. God gave the Philistines hemorrhoids as an indication that they were operating under man-made worship and not worship in spirit and truth. Prophetically, he gave the hemorrhoids as an indication that their worship wasn't giving them access to his Presence.

Don't let me lose you right here; although this may seem a little grotesque, it will help us understand false worship. Ultimately it will all make sense.

Hemorrhoids are veins in the anal area both inside and out. It is a group of skin tissues that form a bulge outside the anal area as a result of these veins being irritated and swollen, and this causes pain, itching, bleeding, and burning sensations. Needless to say, it makes it very painful when you're sitting on the throne attempting to release yourself!

Now remember, hemorrhoids were a condition given to the Philistines by God as an indication that their worship wasn't gaining access to His Presence.

Hemorrhoids are often caused by a bad diet and straining on the toilet, among other things. This is where we get the lesson in all of this.

The problem of hemorrhoids is experienced painfully when we should have a bowel movement, or when waste is supposed to come out of us, but we're having a hard time passing it or letting go. Okay, I know that is really tough description to consider; now let's take it to the spiritual plane.

Spiritual hemorrhoids come from seasons in which we're having a hard time letting go of weight, waste, and sin: stuff that's inside of us that God has revealed to us that we don't need. As a result of straining, a hemorrhoid forms—extra tissue, *extra flesh*; as a result of this extra flesh, every bowel movement is extremely painful. From a spiritual perspective, every time God tells you it's time for you to let go of something that's no good for you, it hurts you. It's painful.

With God's Presence You Have No Problem Letting Go of Stuff

When you're operating under man-made worship, letting go of stuff is a struggle. It's painful to let go of waste—to let go of stuff, people, attitudes, and dysfunctional mind-sets that God has clearly shown he wants you to let go of. The reason there are so many people in the church struggling with deliverance from bondages, yet remaining bound, is because they're seeking liberty in the wrong place. They are not in God's Presence but a man-made manipulated heavenly presence that brings no true deliverance.

The kingdom call is a call to a lifestyle of letting go. "More than that, I now regard all things as liabilities compared to the far greater value of knowing Christ Jesus my Lord, for whom I have suffered the loss of all things—indeed, I regard them as dung!—that I may gain Christ" (Phil. 3:8 NET). When we're truly not accessing God, we'll struggle with God to hold onto things he's given us the release to let go of.

"Let us therefore come boldly unto the throne of grace, that we may obtain mercy, and find grace to help in the time of need" (Heb. 4:16). What we must understand is that we can't be in God's Presence, we can't be worshipping the true and living God, and have hemorrhoids. When truly in God's Presence, we won't have any problem letting go of what God considers waste. When we truly seek God's grace, we receive what we need.

The Bible declares that when John the Revelator came into the presence of the glorified Christ, he fell like a dead man before him. Parts of us that are not like God will die in us as we come into contact with his holy Presence! Just being in God's Presence will kill addictions. Just being in God's Presence will kill bad habits. Just being in God's Presence will kill unforgiveness. When we're really in God's Presence, we don't strain to let go, but we obtain mercy and we find grace to help in the time of need.

Everywhere the Philistines attempted to take the ark—first to Ashdod, then Gath, and finally Ekron-plagues of hemorrhoids broke out against the inhabitants of that city. So the Philistine wise men devised a plan to get rid of the ark. If we pay close attention to that plan, it will help us understand how those who truly experience the Presence of the Lord respond to him.

> Now build a new cart. And find two cows that have just given birth to calves. Make sure the calves have never been yoked to a cart. Hitch the cows to the cart, but shut their calves away from them in a pen. Put the Ark of the Lord on the cart, and beside it place a chest containing the gold rats and gold tumors you are sending as a guilt offering. Then let the cows go wherever they want. If they cross the border of our land and go to Beth-shemesh, we will know it was the Lord who brought this great disaster upon us. If they don't, we will know it was not his hand that caused the plague. It came simply by chance. So these instructions were carried out. Two cows were hitched to the cart, and their newborn calves were shut up in a pen. Then the Ark of the Lord and the chest containing the gold rats and gold tumors were placed on the cart. And sure enough, without veering off in other directions, the cows went straight along the road toward Beth-shemesh (1 Sam. 6:7–12 NLT).

The priests and wise men of Dagon decide to find two cows that had just recently given birth, in order to see if because of the ark, or because of God's Presence being placed on a cart that they're hitched to, they'd be willing to leave their newborns in the stocks without looking back. The Bible declares that because these two cows were pulling God's Presence, they were willing to let go even of their own babies and not look back.

That's when you truly know that you've experienced the Presence of an Almighty God, when you walk away from that thing God has told you to let go of and you never look back! It's not a struggle, strain, or inner battle to walk away from anything that's outside of God's will for your life, because you're carrying the Presence of God! After being in the Presence of God, you recognize that what you let go of is base, insignificant, and wasteful in comparison to walking in God's divine purpose for your life. You won't catch spiritual hemorrhoids. You have no problem letting go of stuff.

Once we truly encounter the Presence of God, like the cows who walked away from their newborns, we will walk away from our own family members if their influence is taking us in a direction contrary to the direction of God for our lives (see Mark 3:33–35). "If you want to be my disciple, you must hate everyone else by comparison—your father and mother, wife and children, brothers and sisters—yes, even your own life. Otherwise, you cannot be my disciple" (Luke 14:26 NLT).

Chapter 14

Worship That Ushers In God's Presence

We Can't Replace the Presence of God with the Presence of Man

After the fall of Saul and his sons, David ascended to the throne of Israel. He was eventually anointed king over all of Israel. In type, he was consecrated pastor and shepherd over God's people. After David was established as the head, the very first legislation as commander and chief was to have God's people go after the ark, where there was the Presence of God. "Let us gather, and let us bring again the ark of our God to us: for we enquired not at it in the days of Saul" (1 Chron. 13:2–3).

David said that in all the days that Saul was king they never went after the Presence of God. What's profound is that in the account in First Samuel, right after Israel lost the ark in chapter 4 they turned around in chapter 8 and asked for a king. Instead of attempting to go after the ark, instead of pursuing the Presence of God, they settled for the presence of man. It speaks prophetically of what's taking place in droves in today's church. There are so many people who have foregone God's Presence and substituted the presence of their pastor or their bishop.

Don't get me wrong—we are to honor and have the utmost respect for those God has called to be his voice in our lives. But we are to never allow being in their presence to replace our personal and private pursuit of the Presence of God. Leaders must be honored and submitted to, because God uses them as a bridge between us and what he desires to release and impart into us. We shouldn't, however, allow revivals, convocations, and public meetings and the presence we experience there to replace our walking with God daily. I truly believe that we're living in a Saul generation in which many in the church are going to be so caught up into going to see "Prophet so-and-so" speak or "Evangelist such-and-much" preach when they come to town that they are going to miss Jesus when he comes.

David represents true kingdom leadership. The first thing any true kingdom leader will tell you is not to go after your dreams, your breakthrough, or your blessing, but instead to go after his Presence! In the gospel of Luke, when the angel Gabriel prophesies about the birth of Jesus unto Mary, he says that *Jesus will sit on the throne of David* (Luke 1:32). In other words, Jesus makes his habitation on David's throne. David's throne, his kingship, was founded on one thing: pursuing God's Presence.

If we're going to find God and experience his Presence, we're going to find him sitting on David's throne. We're going to have to set ourselves to pursue God's Presence! David's throne typifies a perpetual pursuit of God's Presence. We find God by pursuing God. We stay in a place of perpetual presence as we stay in a place of perpetual pursuit. God's Presence is only guaranteed for God chasers. Although when you chase God you'll find him, you've got to keep chasing him if you're going to keep finding him!

It Was the Oxen's Fault, Not Uzzah's

As David sets out to bring the ark of God (and thereby the Presence of God) back to Israel, his actions give us prophetic insight on what we can and can't do in worship to usher in the true Presence of God.

> And they carried the ark of God in a new cart out of the house of Abinadab: and Uzzah and Ahio drove the cart ... And when they came unto the threshing floor of Chi'don, Uzzah put forth his hand to hold the ark; for the oxen stumbled. And the anger of the Lord was kindled against Uzzah, and he smote him, because he put his hand to the Ark; and there he died before the Lord (1 Chron. 13:7–10).

Many times, I believe, we miss the revelation of this text because we focus so much on Uzzah putting his hand on the ark and ignore the reason why he did it: the ox that was carrying it stumbled at the threshing floor!

Jesus Died to Kill the Animal in Us

To understand the ox, we've got to look at the fact that all throughout the Old Testament Scripture, God ordained for his people to give animal sacrifice as the covering for their sins. From the days of Moses up to the sacrifice of Christ, it was God's will that his people sacrifice animals to cover their sins. Hebrews 9:12–13 makes it clear that *the blood of these animals couldn't remove our sins, but only cover them.* This means that the one giving the animal sacrifice would go back and yet live in sin after the blood of the animal was shed on their behalf. Jesus's blood is the only entity that can remove the sinful nature so that we can serve God. The question is, If that is indeed the case, why did God ordain the slaughter of hundreds of thousands of animals for sacrifices before he came and gave the actual and true sacrifice?

God is not a wasteful God. He didn't waste these animals' lives. I believe God was trying to speak to us prophetically through those sacrifices about what he was going to do through Jesus, the ultimate sacrifice. Through Jesus's sacrifice, God was killing the animal in us! He was killing the untamed part of us! He was mortifying that wild nature in us! The undomesticated natural man in us that desires to do what it wants to do, when it wants to do it! Please understand that Satan was a serpent in the garden. When Adam sinned, he took on the nature of Satan, an animal. So the natural man is actually the animal part of man.

Animals are wild creatures that live by their own instincts. Some might be domesticated, but they can never be completely tamed. Animals can't submit themselves to the rules of civilized living. Before we were saved, we couldn't submit ourselves to God and his law. "Because the outlook of the flesh [the unsaved and unregenerate] is hostile to God, for it does not submit to the law of God, nor is it able to do so" (Rom. 8:7–8 NET). The inability to submit is a trait that comes directly from animals. Being rebellious is being animalistic!

The letter of Jude speaks of unregenerate men behaving as animals: "Yet these men, as a result of their dreams, defile the flesh, reject authority, and insult the glorious ones … But these men do not understand the things that they slander, and they are being destroyed by the very things that, like irrational animals, they try to comprehend instinctively" (Jude v. 8, 10 NET).

The Ox Is Prophetic for Believers Who Haven't Mortified the Animal within Them

The story of the ox speaks prophetically of believers who haven't allowed the cross to deal with all of the animal in them. It speaks of believers who are yet working through the rebellious hardheadedness within themselves.

From a prophetic perspective, David's problem was that he was trying to get ox-headed, stubborn, and rebellious people to carry the Presence of God. The problem comes when this ox—who in type represents a believer who is yet mortifying the defiance, the animal, in him—gets to the threshing floor.

On the threshing floor, after stalks of grain had been cut, it was necessary to separate out the kernels from the stalk, or the wheat from the tare, before the wheat could be ground into flour. Threshing floors would be used for large amounts of grain, which were open, exposed areas, of rocky hard ground.

The threshing floor is prophetic for the hard place. The sheaves would be laid on the floor, and the kernels were crushed out of the tare by the hooves of the ox. The threshing floor represents the place of crushing, the place of separation. The hard places God allows us to go through to be crushed, so he can separate the wheat and tare in us, the spirit and flesh in us, the natural man from the spiritual man. Without the crush, we'll never be able to separate what's in us that's good and what's in us that's evil, what's in us that God can use and what he can't use.

When the ox got to the threshing floor, the place of crushing, the place of perfection, the place of separation unto God, the Bible declares that he started stumbling. In other words he began "trippin'." The ox started trippin' when he was brought to the place of sanctification. The ox started dropping God.

The threshing floor is the place where the stalks of wheat that have already been harvested (the believers that have already come to Christ) are crushed, are stepped on, and are walked on, so that the wheat and tare can be separated. Even after we're saved from our sin, we still as believers have to go through threshing floor seasons, seasons in which God crushes us to deal with the parts of us that he can't use. At salvation, God accepts us, even though he can't use all of us, because he knows that he can sift us. When we say yes to Jesus, we're also saying yes to the threshing floor! God will take us as we are, but he sure won't leave us as we are!

Unregenerate Man Will Always Start "Trippin'"
When God Is Dealing with Him

Prophetically, the ox started trippin' when God started dealing with him. Oxen in Scripture are a symbol of pride and strength. They're defiant animals.

Bulls are oxen. When bulls see red (when they see the blood), they don't bow to it, they charge at it! Bulls have a problem with submission! Bull-headed saints don't have a problem with the blood saving them; they have a problem with the blood demanding their total submission. The reason why rodeo shows, in which cowboys get on top of bulls and ride them, are so entertaining is because bulls don't like to let anything get on top of them. Bulls don't like to be underneath anything. David's problem was that he was attempting to get God to play ride 'em cowboy on a bull (believer with an unrenewed mind) that was yet to learn how to be underneath legitimate authority!

The ox began trippin' when God started dealing with him—and dropped the ark. The ox started dropping God. When God is dealing with those not yet delivered from the animal in them, they'll drop their church attendance at the threshing floor. They'll drop their consecration at the threshing floor. They'll drop their commitment to pay tithe and offering at the threshing floor.

It wasn't Uzzah's fault that he died—it was David's fault for believing that an ox could carry God's Presence. The reason why God's Presence isn't coming in and moving in our gatherings like the Bible testifies that it will is because we're entrusting too many people with ministry who haven't yet dealt with all of the animal in themselves! So every time they come to a threshing floor experience, the first thing that they drop is ministry! The first thing they drop is the church when they're in tribulation. They don't recognize their tribulation as an opportunity to usher in the kingdom of God. *We must go through many tribulations to enter into the kingdom of God.*

God Killed Uzzah for Trying to Keep His Presence on Someone Who Was Trippin'

When the ox begins trippin', and begins dropping the Presence of God, Uzzah places his hand on the ark so that God's Presence could remain on the ox. God strikes Uzzah dead for trying to keep his Presence on someone who doesn't understand that it's too valuable to drop. God refuses to remain on anyone who trips at the threshing floor, because the threshing floor is necessary to properly carry him.

I believe that this is the reason why so many pastors, elders, and leaders are dying spiritually, throwing in the towel, closing their churches, and giving up on ministry. So many pastors are stressed out, burned out, and exhausted with the work of God because they, like Uzzah, try to keep God's Presence on people who will drop it every time it inconveniences them.

Pastors are dying by the multitudes on the threshing floor! All because in their anxiousness to bring to pass the vision given to them by God, they place the weight of God's Presence on oxen instead of waiting for God to send them Levites!

So instead of focusing on ministries that carry God's Presence into the community, the neighborhoods, and those who are in need within the city, the pastor spends all of his time placing and replacing God's Presence upon the backs of a people who are yet to be delivered from self! Such a pastor winds up dying trying to balance the ark on a bunch of oxen. Instead of taking the time to cultivate in the people a broken and contrite heart toward the Lord, in an unsanctified haste, this leadership attempts to place God's Presence on an unbroken people.

We've Got to Be under God's Hand to Be in God's Presence

To carry the ark speaks of submission. The ark was on top of the ox. The ox was under the cart which held God's Presence. In order to be in position to carry the presence of God, you've got to be willing to be under somebody! God's Presence is inextricably tied to your relationship to God's servants. If you're not willing to be under God's servants, you don't qualify to carry God's Presence. Saints that aren't delivered from self can't get past themselves.

> Likewise you younger people submit yourselves to your elders. Yes, all of you be submissive to one another, and be clothed with humility, for "God resists the proud, But gives grace to the humble. Therefore humble yourselves under the mighty hand of God, that He may exalt you in due time (1 Peter 5:5–6 NKJV).

Notice that the first of these verses talks about being submissive to one another, or humbling yourselves under one another, while the next talks about humbling yourself under God. Why? Because the two are inseparable. You can't humble yourself unto God without humbling yourself under godly leadership, and you can't humble yourself under godly leadership without humbling yourself unto God. If you truly desire to submit yourself to the Word and will of God, you will submit to leadership. There is no way around it. God's Presence is only for those who don't have a problem being underneath someone. We must humble ourselves under God's mighty hand, five-fold ministry: the apostle, prophet, evangelist, pastor, and teacher (Eph. 4:11). God's hand is five-fold ministry! His hand is his servants.

Those who are ox-headed will cast off God's delegated authority when they're on the threshing floor--not understanding that by casting off delegated authority, they cast off God's Presence. By coming out from under spiritual authority, they are separated from the Presence of God. God's people and God's Presence are tied together.

We can see this through Jesus's actions as he rode on the donkey in his final entrance into Jerusalem.

Covering and Communion with God Go Hand in Hand—Once You Allow Someone to Cover You, God Will Sit on You

> And when they came nigh to Jerusalem, unto Bethany, at the mount of Olives, he sendeth forth two of his disciples and saith unto them, Go your way into the village over against you: and as soon as ye entered into it, ye shall find a colt tied, whereon never man sat; loose him, and bring him … And they brought the colt to Jesus, and cast their garments on him; and Jesus sat upon him (Mark 11:1–2, 7).

The disciples untied the donkey in verse 2, and Jesus turned around and sat on the donkey in verse 7. We can't overlook that, because there is a divine revelation here. This wild animal, this donkey, had just been untied—prophetically, he had just been delivered. He had just been set free. He was just a babe in Christ, and he had just gotten disconnected from what was keeping him from his purpose for Jesus. He had gotten saved in verse 2, and Jesus sat on him in verse 7. It took him five verses to move from salvation to purpose.

We can't overlook the prophetic symbol of Jesus sitting on this donkey. The act of sitting is significant here, and in some other places in the Bible as well. John the Baptist knew that Jesus was the Son of God because, after being baptized, the Holy Spirit came down in the form of a dove and sat on Jesus. And later, when the day of Pentecost had fully come, the Holy Spirit came in the form of cloven tongues of fire: "And there appeared unto them cloven tongues like as a fire, and sat upon each of them" (Acts 2:3). After Jesus sat down on the right hand of the Father, he poured out the spirit of God. In the Scripture, the action of sitting is a symbol of being filled with the Spirit of God! It is carrying God's Presence, walking with God's Presence. It speaks of God's Presence staying on you. This donkey got untied in verse 2, and was carrying the Presence of God in verse 7. Why?

The Bible says, in verse 7, that *the apostles cast their garments on the donkey, and then Jesus sat on him.* Jesus sat on him, right after the disciples covered him! That donkey had to let Jesus's servants cover him before Jesus would sit on him! Once you allow God's delegated authority to cover you, God will sit on you.

If Jesus is sitting on you, it's because somebody is covering you. Maybe that's why there are so many folks in the house of God who aren't filled with the Holy Spirit and walking with the Presence of God—because we can't have Jesus sitting on us uncovered. So many saints don't have any power, because so many saints don't have any cover. Only those who are covered enjoy abiding in God's Presence. They enjoy continuously walking with God, in constant communion with him, and being led by the Spirit.

We need God's Presence in order to walk in the Spirit. Once Jesus sat on the donkey, the donkey only went in the direction that Jesus wanted him to go. He was led by the Spirit! There are too many believers that believe they can cast off their covering without casting off God's Presence. But the two are inseparable.

Only the Levites Can Carry God's Presence

> And David made him houses in the city of David, and prepared a place for the ark of God, and pitched for it a tent. Then David said, None ought to carry the ark of God but the Levites; for them hath the Lord chosen to carry the ark of God, and to minister unto him forever ... And said unto them, ye are the chief of the fathers of the Levites: sanctify yourselves, both ye and your brethren, that you may bring up the ark of the Lord God of Israel unto the place that I have prepared for it ... And the children of the Levites bare the ark of God upon their shoulders with the staves thereon as Moses commanded according to the word of the Lord (1 Chron. 15:1–2, 12–15).

David makes it clear that the reason God broke out against Israel the first time, striking Uzzah dead, was because they had an ox carrying God's Presence instead of a Levite. David said that the Levites were chosen to carry God's Presence. *Many are called but few are chosen.* God's Presence can't be carried by oxen or by those who trip on the threshing floor or at the place of submission and sacrifice, but only those who have been chosen can carry the glory. The qualification for carrying God's Presence was being a son of Levi, a Levite. We can't miss that, because that speaks to us prophetically about those who qualify to usher God's Presence back into the house of God.

Levi was the third son of Jacob. When Leah birthed him she said, "Now this time will my husband be joined unto me, because I have born him three sons: therefore was his name called Levi" (Gen. 29:34). Levi means joined. Prophetically, the Levites speak of those who are joined, connected, and in true fellowship with no schisms, cliques, divisions, or selfish motives. Ephesians says, "From Jesus the whole body, joined and held together by every supporting ligament, grows and builds itself up in love, as each part does is work" (Eph. 4:16 NIV).

Only Levites, only those who were truly joined, could carry the ark, the Presence of the Lord, because of the way in which they had to carry it. The ark was a small chest which was four feet long, two feet wide, and two feet high. Four Levites were to carry the ark together, on their shoulders, by way of four staves placed through grooves in each of the four corners of the ark. Because the ark was so small, the only way that the Levites could carry it was by being close to one another. They had to carry the ark together.

They had to remain in step and in unity with one another. They couldn't be worried about getting ahead of one another or trying to be more blessed and anointed than one another. They had to be Levites; they had to be joined. The only way they could carry God's Presence was if they remained close.

We can't be joined in order to *get* God's Presence; we've got to be joined before we *receive* God's Presence. In order for the Levites to keep God's Presence on their shoulders, they had to remain close to one another. If we're truly going to carry the Presence of God, we've got to love our brothers like we love God, because we must recognize that if we drop our brother, we also have to drop God! If one of the four Levites carrying the ark decided he no longer wanted to be in relationship with one of the other Levites and got out of relationship with them, he would have to walk away from God's ark (Presence) as well.

For Levites, the one thing that keeps them connected is God's Presence. So no matter how much you hurt me, I've got to forgive you for the sake of God's Presence! No matter what the misunderstanding we have no other choice but to work through it, for the sake of God's Presence. If we ever stop fighting and contending for the unity of the faith, we literally stop fighting and contending for the Presence of God. God's Presence can only be carried by those who are in true divine fellowship and connection.

There are so many ministries that are operating in a pseudo-presence of God because they emphasize presentation over personification. They believe that God's Presence hinges on them presenting good sounding praise teams and choirs, orderly inviting services, and nice looking facilities. The problem is you can have all these things, and yet lack the Presence of God. God doesn't want presentation, he wants personification. God wants us, as a group of believers to personify Christ. Christ is one! "Hear O' Israel, the Lord thy God is one Lord" (Deut. 6:4).

God desires for us to be one in the spirit. You can have order in the natural and total chaos in the spirit. There are many churches that have a presentation that looks orderly in the natural, but are in total chaos and division in the spirit. They put on a good presentation, but behind the scenes of ministry people are jealous of one another, competing with one another, upset and not talking to one another, and just plan frustrated with one another. But as long as what they're doing draws crowds and looks well, all of these things are overlooked by the church. Without realizing it, they put on a great presentation that lacks God's Presence, because God's Presence can only be ushered in by those who are in true spiritual unity.

"God desires truth in the inward parts" (Ps. 51:6). Not just in the inward parts of us as individual believers, but in the inward parts of the corporate body. God desires truth in the inward workings of ministry. It profits us nothing before God, how we look on the outside, if we're not walking in the truth of unity in the inward workings of ministry. His Presence won't rest upon the shoulders of our work, and we'll have to act like God is there when he's really not!

Unity Must Be Carried Full Term

> So David went and brought up the ark of God from the house of Obed-edom into the city of David with gladness. And it was so, that when they that bare the ark of the Lord had gone six paces, he sacrificed oxen and fatlings (2 Sam. 6:12–13).

David and the Levites had to carry the ark, God's Presence from the city of Kir'jath-je'a-rim to Jerusalem. This city was nine miles north of Jerusalem. The Levites had to walk in unity, they had to stay connected, or remain joined for nine miles in order to bring God's glory back home. Nine is a prophetic number. It's the number of birthing. A woman is supposed to carry a child for nine months in order to give birth. I believe that God is saying prophetically that if we as a church could carry unity for nine months in our local churches, we would see the Glory and Presence of God like never before.

If we wouldn't allow the Enemy to come in and use slander, offense, and lies to divide us for nine months, God's glory would come in to heal, deliver, destroy yokes, and add souls to the church daily. The Enemy continues to attack us with a spirit that divides us, and cause us to abort the glory, presence of God, and move of God that he's impregnated us with. God's assignment to us is to carry unity for nine months, and the glory that he'll release we'll be reaping for nine years.

We Must Be a Living Sacrifice in Order to Carry God's Presence

The Bible declares that every six paces, which is about eighteen feet, the Levites, David, and all of Israel would stop and sacrifice one bull and one fatted calf. What is so profound about this, and what does it speak to us about worship that ushers in the presence of the Lord?

There are about 5,280 feet in one mile, they walked with the ark for nine miles, which means they had to travel 47,520 feet. They would literally stop every eighteen feet and give God a sacrifice in order to usher God's Presence back into Jerusalem. This means they stopped 2,640 times to sacrifice unto God, just to carry God's Presence nine miles! David sacrificed one bull and one fatted calf 2,640 times. It means he had to give God 5,280 sacrifices to walk with his Presence for nine miles! That's why there are so few people who can actually usher in the Presence of God through worship, because his true divine Presence can only be brought in through sacrifice!

To walk with and usher in God's Presence, we can't *give* a sacrifice; we must *be* a living sacrifice. To walk with God's Presence we can't be in a hurry. "Through faith and patience we inherit the promises of God" (Heb. 6:12).

I'm sure that as David and the Levites, as well as Israel, carried the ark, stopping every six paces or eighteen feet, the temptation arose to get weary with the walk, simply because it was taking them such a long time to travel what seemed to be such a short distance. A distance they could have completed a lot faster had they not been carrying the Presence of God. Many ministries have fallen to the temptation of focusing more on getting to where they're going than maintaining God's Presence. In the body of Christ we've got to realize, that it's not so much about where we're going but about making sure we still have God's Presence when we get there!

When God was about to give Israel the Promised Land without his Presence, Moses replied, "If your Presence does not go with us, do not send us up from here" (Ex. 33:15 TNIV). I say, sadly, that many ministries have taken the deal of having their promises without God's true Shekinah Presence going with them! I'm sure there was the temptation for many of those walking with the ark to feel like they really weren't going anywhere, but the Levites yet stayed together, and carried the ark. In ministry we've got to be willing to remain together even though it doesn't seem like we're going anywhere. We've got to be willing to sacrifice, even when it seems like our sacrifice isn't taking us anywhere. As long as we maintain God's Presence within what we're doing, eventually we'll get to our promise.

CONCLUSION

As I bring this prophetic word to a close, my prayer is that you will hear the voice of God in it. I know it's not mainstream, I know it's not what's popularly being taught, but it is indeed the voice of the Lord. If you heard God's prophetic cry out of this book, I want you to understand that you will be held accountable by God himself for what you know. You must be a good steward over the knowledge God has given you. You must set yourself to give what you've received. "My people are destroyed for lack of knowledge" (Hos. 4:6).

If the words in this work set your heart aflame and woke or stirred something up inside of you, it's because God at this very moment is calling you to be a prophetic messenger and watchman in this last and evil day. You can no longer push God's call and summons aside. You have been enlisted! Yes it's going to cost you. Yes, you're going to have to walk away from some people, organizations, and family. Yes, many won't like you because of the message God has given you. But the body of Christ is depending on you answering the call of a prophetic watchman. You have no choice! As I close, I leave you with Ezekiel 33:2–9 (with my emphasis added to some of the sentences):

> Son of man, speak to the children of thy people, and say unto them, When I bring the sword upon a land, if the people of the land take a man of their coasts, and set him for their watchman: If when he seeth the sword come upon the land, he blow the trumpet, and warn the people; then whosoever heareth the sound of the trumpet, and taketh not warning; if the sword come, and take him away, his blood shall be upon his own head. He heard the sound of the trumpet, and took not warning; his blood shall be upon him. But he that taketh warning shall deliver his soul. *But if the watchman see the sword come, and blow not the trumpet, and the people be not warned; if the sword come, and take any*

person from among them, he is taken away in his iniquity; but his blood will I require at the watchman's hand. So thou, O son of man, I have set thee a watchman unto the house of Israel; therefore thou shalt hear the word at my mouth, and warn them from me. *When I say unto the wicked, O wicked man, thou shalt surely die; if thou dost not speak to warn the wicked from his way, that wicked man shall die in his iniquity; but his blood will I require at thine hand.* Nevertheless, if thou warn the wicked of his way to turn from it; if he does not turn from his way, he shall die in his iniquity; but thou hast delivered thy soul.